Digital Transformation Systems & Enterprise Platform Modernization

Manisha Ponugoti

Sandeepa Genne

notionpress.com

INDIA • SINGAPORE • MALAYSIA

ISBN

Paperback 979-8-90431-543-6
Hardcase 979-8-90431-544-3

Contents

2. ENTERPRISE ARCHITECTURE AND PLATFORM MODERNIZATION

3. DIGITAL TECHNOLOGIES FOR ENTERPRISE TRANSFORMATION

5. VALUE MEASUREMENT AND FUTURE ENTERPRISE PLATFORMS

Preface

Digital transformation is no longer a strategic option—it is a business imperative. Organizations across industries are reimagining their operations, customer experiences, and value delivery models through the integration of advanced technologies and modern enterprise platforms. *Digital Transformation Systems & Enterprise Platform Modernization* is designed to provide a structured and practical understanding of how enterprises can navigate this complex journey.

This book explores foundational concepts, architectural frameworks, modernization strategies, and emerging technology trends that shape the future of digital enterprises. It bridges the gap between business vision and technical execution, offering insights for students, professionals, and decision-makers alike. Our goal is to equip readers with the knowledge and tools needed to build resilient, scalable, and future-ready systems in an ever-evolving digital landscape.

Dedication

We dedicate this book to all innovators, learners, and professionals who strive to transform ideas into impactful digital solutions.

To our families, whose unwavering support and encouragement made this work possible.

And to the global community of technology enthusiasts who continue to push the boundaries of what is possible in the digital era.

Acknowledgement

We express our sincere gratitude to everyone who contributed to the development of this book.

We thank our mentors, colleagues, and industry experts whose insights and experiences have significantly shaped the perspectives presented here. Their guidance has been invaluable in bringing clarity and depth to complex topics.

We also acknowledge the contributions of the broader technology community, whose continuous innovation and shared knowledge inspire ongoing learning and growth.

Finally, we extend our heartfelt thanks to our families and friends for their patience, encouragement, and constant support throughout this journey.

Chapter 1
Foundations of Digital Transformation

1.1 OVERVIEW

Digital transformation requires organizations to completely transform their operations through technology which helps them create value and maintain their operations and develop new business strategies. The process requires organizations to adopt digital tools while also transforming their business models and enterprise structures and governance systems and organizational culture. The current business environment shows how organizations have advanced from using basic automation to creating complete operational systems which help them compete and work together and provide services in today's data-driven world.

The chapter establishes the essential conceptual elements together with strategic elements which help people grasp digital transformation systems and enterprise platform modernization. The research investigates fundamental definitions which drive business competition while examining new technological innovations and digital maturity assessment systems and obstacles to modernization which arise from outdated systems and existing technical debt. The chapter establishes a structured framework which combines technological organizational and strategic elements to help readers investigate enterprise architecture and platform modernization in upcoming sections.

1.1.1 Historical Evolution of Enterprise Digitalization

The historical development of enterprise digitalization is a manifestation of the gradual introduction of information technologies into the structure, organization processes, and strategies. The first half of the 1960s until the end of the 1970s restricted its development to automatic processing of standard data operations. The primary applications of mainframe systems included accounting and payroll and inventory management which improved computation performance without affecting corporate strategic decisions. Digital systems at this level operated as support systems for operations but did not function as systems that enabled strategic development.

This transformation occurred during the 1980s and 1990s when companies began using their complete operations through Enterprise Resource Planning (ERP) systems and Customer Relationship Management (CRM) systems and Supply Chain Management (SCM) platforms. The integrated systems established direct connections between different functions while creating unified standards that all departments had to follow. The internet created better links between companies which enabled them to perform electronic trading and electronic communications and manage their worldwide supply chains. Digitalization began its transition from hidden IT implementation work to complete enterprise integration and value chain optimization processes.

Digital technologies began to establish their role in strategic decision-making processes during the early 2000s. The combination of data analytics and web-based platforms and mobile technologies enabled organizations to enhance customer engagement while improving operational flexibility. Cloud computing emerged as a solution that removed infrastructure limitations to provide organizations with flexible and scalable IT resources. The digitalization process reached a point where organizations used it to improve their internal operations and develop new business models and establish ecosystem partnerships and build service delivery networks.

The modern world is marked by the digitalization of enterprises, platform-based architecture, artificial intelligence, real-time analytics, and connected digital ecosystems. Digital transformation is no longer being associated with technological uptake but covers cultural shift, redesigning of the organization and an ongoing innovation. Organizations are currently working in digitally enabled value networks in which data is becoming a strategic resource. This historical trend shows that digitalization of enterprises has been developed in the context of operational automation to an extensive, strategy-oriented transformation of the creation of competitive advantage and long-term sustainability (Ahmed, 2024).

1.1.2 Definitional Debates and Conceptual Boundaries

The idea of digital transformation is the focus of intense academic discussion, though the agreement on defining what exactly it is has not been reached yet. Information systems, strategic management, organizational theory, and the study of innovation are the various disciplinary approaches that have influenced a wide range of interpretations in academic literature. Other researchers define digital transformation as a process where advanced digital technologies are introduced into business processes, but some also focus more on the overall organizational and strategic effects of the digital transformation. This descriptive plurality has added to the existing arguments on the conceptual range and limits of the word.

The first point of confusion is that the similar terms of digitization, digitalization, and digital transformation are used interchangeably. Digitization is usually understood as transformation of analog data into digital form, but the digitalization term is applied to refer to the application of digital technologies that can be used to improve or redesign business processes. Digital transformation, conversely, does not focus on process improvement only, but includes essential changes in the organization structure, value creation logic, different forms of interacting with customers, and competitive positioning. Such distinctions should be clarified to prevent conceptual vagueness and overlap of analysis.

The other controversy is whether the digital transformation should be perceived as an organizational change process that is driven by strategies or as a technology-driven phenomenon. Technology-oriented views are based on the use of innovations like cloud computing, artificial intelligence, and platform architectures. The difference here brings out the socio-technical aspect of change wherein humans, organization, and technology interact dynamically. The informational limits of the digital transformation also have an extension to the issues of size and intensity. There are interpretations that it is a gradual, steady enhancement by constantly integrating digitally, and others that refer to it as a disruptive and radical re-organization of enterprise functioning (Richards, 2015).

1.1.3 Digital Transformation as a Socio-Technical Phenomenon

Digital transformation is becoming more and more recognized not only as a technological enhancement but also as a socio-technical phenomenon that captures the interplay between technology, human beings, organizational forms and institutional settings. Business organizations that adopt digital transformation initiatives should also ensure that they focus on the technology potential and human, cultural, and organizational aspects. This perspective demonstrates that successful transformation requires organizations to adopt advanced digital technologies while establishing new methods for their workforce to work together and create value within digital environments.

The digital transformation process combines technical infrastructure elements which include cloud-based technologies and data mining tools and automation technologies with social infrastructure components which encompass workforce proficiency and leadership practices and corporate culture and stakeholder relationship management. The online programs achieve their efficiency through the combined operation of technical elements and social elements which exist as two separate components. Organizations that implement technology without assessing their workers' readiness and their organization's ability to adapt to new processes face resistance and fail to adopt new systems and achieve minimal organizational changes.

Digital transformation through the socio-technical perspective changes power structures within organizations which affects decision-making processes and communication patterns. Organizations need to establish data-driven decision-making processes which require employees to develop fresh competencies while leaders must cultivate an innovative environment that values experimentation and supports continuous education. Also, the digital transformation strategies are shaped by external socio-economic conditions, such as regulatory frameworks, market anticipations, and industry ecologies (Schwertner, 2025).

Important Areas of Digital Transformation as a Socio-Technical Phenomenon.

Technological Dimension: Organizations use digital technology through three main processes which include both implementation of digital systems and their actual use in their operations to achieve maximum results.

- Modernization to high-end digital infrastructure.
- Combination of information-driven systems and automation.
- Creation of scalable and adjustable online systems.

Human and Workforce Dimension: The human aspect of the study examines how digital transformation affects employee skills, their work habits, and their ability to work with others, while studying the organizational learning capacity of the organization.

- Development of skills and improvement of digital literacy.
- Employees flexibility and readiness to change.
- Cooperation in digitally facilitated workplaces.

Organizational Dimension: The organizational aspect requires three elements which include structural changes and cultural changes together with necessary process changes for sustaining digital transformation initiatives.

- Business process and workflow transformation.
- Development of leadership and governing models.
- Development of innovation-related organizational cultures.

Strategic Dimension: In terms of strategy, focus refers to the adjustment of digital efforts with long term business objectives, competitive positioning, and value creation processes.

- Harmonization of digital programs with business plan.
- Online business model development.
- Digital ecosystems to create values in the long term.

Environmental and Ecosystem Dimension: This dimension assesses how external elements, which include regulatory frameworks and industry competition and market dynamics and ecosystem connections, shape digital transformation processes.

- Influences of regulatory and compliance.
- Competition in the industry and digital disruption.
- Platform-based and partner networks collaboration.

Organizations need to understand digital transformation through its socio-technical aspects because this approach provides them with complete knowledge to handle their complex transformation needs. The research shows that companies achieve lasting digital success through their requirement to establish a system which integrates technology, staff members and business objectives.

1.2 DIGITAL TRANSFORMATION CONCEPTS

The process of employing technology to turn traditional company operations and procedures into digital systems is known as digital transformation. The organization needs to implement modern technologies which include big data analytics and cloud computing and artificial intelligence in order to achieve better performance results and improved operational efficiency. Digital transformation is more than just leveraging technology. The organization needs to update its operational procedures and business models and organizational culture to achieve better results. The organization needs to maintain ongoing communication with its clients while understanding their needs to achieve exceptional service delivery through digital transformation.

Digital Transformation's Significance:

- **Increasing the Effectiveness of Operations:** Businesses achieve heightened operational efficiency through digital transformation which uses process automation and waste elimination methods. The process leads to decreased costs and faster operational results.
- **Improving the Client Experience:** Digital transformation services help businesses achieve their goal of delivering exceptional customer experiences. Businesses use technological tools to divide their target audience into specific groups, which helps them build stronger connections and interact with customers more effectively. Businesses can achieve higher customer satisfaction and better customer retention rates through technology that delivers personalized experiences to their clients. The company must deliver timely and effective solutions that meet customer requirements.
- **Aiding in the Making of Decisions:** Digital transformation enables organizations to collect and analyze data more effectively, which leads to better strategic decisions that rely on accurate information. The data reveals both customer preferences and current market trends.
- **Promoting Innovation:** Digital transformation brings multiple benefits to organizations through its ability to support innovative solutions. The current global business environment demands organizations to maintain pace with technological development and technological progress while managing their workforce through remote work solutions. Adopting technology and services for digital transformation puts your business at the forefront of innovation and guarantees relevance and competitiveness in a business environment that is always changing. Organisations can test new concepts and create cutting-edge goods and services that satisfy consumer demands through digital transformation initiatives.

Enhancing operational efficiency, offering more sophisticated and easily available services, and fostering innovation in a variety of domains are the main objectives of digital transformation. In order to achieve sustainable development, it seeks to enable people and organisations to take full advantage of contemporary technologies in order to save time and effort (RMG, 2025).

Determine what digital means to your practice because every organization will have a different definition of digital transformation. It can occasionally entail abandoning established corporate procedures in favour of more recent ones that are still developing.

Once your aim has been determined and you have decided to implement digital transformation in your organization, it is crucial to keep in mind that, despite the fact that it may seem like a technological change, the core of the notion is leadership and culture. Making this a success requires a shift that is spearheaded from the top and infused with a willingness to master the technology.

It makes sense that the initial transition to new legal technology could be daunting. However, the transition to legal technology can be easy and convenient if skilled and knowledgeable practitioners are leading the way and utilizing solutions that facilitate communication, teamwork, and job management. It is imperative that key performance indicators be established because measuring achievement is essential to sustaining investment. The process would be more favorable moving forward once objectives are met and checkboxes are checked (MyKase, 2026).

1.2.1 Digitization, Digitalization, and Transformation: Conceptual Distinctions

The academic and industrial fields use digitization digitalization and digital transformation as interchangeable terms which create confusion about their actual meanings. The technology adoption process in enterprises consists of three distinct but interconnected stages which developers need to understand to succeed in their work. The digital strategy development process requires researchers and practitioners and policymakers to understand these conceptual distinctions because they need to create efficient digital strategies and evaluate organizational transformation results.

The initial stage of digitization establishes a basic framework which enables organizations to transform all their physical documents into electronic formats. Through digital technologies digitalization enables organizations to enhance their business operations and achieve greater efficiency in their daily functions. Digital transformation describes a complete business transformation which uses digital technologies to develop new customer experiences and business value systems. The three concepts create a maturity continuum which begins with data conversion and ends with complete strategic transformation of the organization.

- **Digitization:** The process of transforming tangible items into digital formats is known as digitization. An example of this would be document scanning, where text from physical paper is converted into PDF or other digital formats, which are then stored in the computer. Information is arranged into bits by digitization. Computers can process, store, and transfer analogue data because it is encoded into zeroes and ones. Digitization is a crucial component of digital technology since it forms the foundation for data recording.
- **Digitalization:** Physical items or information are saved on computers during digitization, but the technique by which this data is used might not be altered. The primary distinction between digitization and digitalization is this. Digital technologies and data are used to facilitate or enhance operations through digitalization. Digitalization is all about creating procedures and altering workflows to enhance manual systems, whereas digitization is primarily about converting and capturing data. Using digital client data from many sources to automatically produce insights from their behaviour is one example of this.
- **Digital Transformation:** Integrating technology into most, if not all, company operations is the main goal of digital transformation, which is closely related to digitization and digitalization. In digital transformation, digital technology is integrated into every aspect of the company to significantly

increase workflow efficiency and add value for clients. Digital technology integration is used to implement organizational, operational, and cultural changes. Businesses can adjust to the constantly shifting landscapes and trends of their industries thanks to digital transformation.

Digitization vs. Digitalization vs. Digital Transformation

The terms "digitalization," "digital transformation," and "digitalization" can be readily confused. These three ideas, however, differ in a number of ways, including their goals and results.

Let's start by talking about the goal and result:

- The goal of digitization is to convert analogue to digital formats in order to encode information in computers. Data recording that may later be utilized in digital technologies is the primary focus of the process.
- Information processing, or how digital data may be used to enhance workflows by automating current procedures, is the focus of digitalization.
- Ultimately, the goal of digital transformation is to increase engagement and generate new value by utilizing knowledge and integrating it across all business domains.

Digitalization creates its essential base through the process of converting data into digital formats. The first process converts data into digital formats while the second process improves operational efficiency through better business operations. Digital transformation leads to complete changes in both organizational structure and strategic direction. Organizations that understand these differences between digital technologies can create effective digital roadmaps while they distribute their resources and choose which technologies to implement for their business needs. These concepts show how businesses evolve to meet digital economy requirements while maintaining their market position and ability to innovate and remain strong in a world that increasingly relies on technology (Monton, 2022).

1.2.2 Digital Business Model Innovation

Digital business model innovation refers to the strategic redesign of how an organization creates, delivers, and captures value in a digital environment. The concept of digital business model innovation extends beyond product and service improvements to require organizations to transform their core business operations according to digital technology advances and changing customer needs and their industry competition. The digital economy requires business models to adapt for mission success because businesses without adaptable business models face obsolescence while companies that develop innovative core business models gain access to new markets and improve their stakeholder value and achieve sustainable growth.

Digital business model innovation needs organizations to implement four specific changes which include developing new value propositions and identifying new customer segments and establishing new revenue streams and implementing new operational methods. The combination of digital platforms and data analytics and connectivity solutions creates fresh opportunities for companies to connect with customers and redesign their product offerings and streamline their value delivery processes. The digital business model innovation uses technology-driven subscription models together with platform ecosystems and data-monetization strategies to transform industry environments (Stähler, 2026).

The art of improving advantage and value generation through concurrent, mutually beneficial changes to an organization's fundamental operational model and value proposition to customers is known as business model innovation. These adjustments can be made at the value proposition level to address the revenue model, product or service offering, and target segment selection. The emphasis at the operating model level is on how to use these choices about how to present the value proposition to increase profitability, competitive advantage, and value creation:

- Where on the value chain should I play?
- Which cost model is required to guarantee profitable returns?

- Which competencies and organizational structure are necessary for success?

Innovation in business models is equally essential to corporate transformation. A number of organisations have similar concerns: What kind of innovation in business models will enable us to reach breakthrough results? How do we keep the core business safe? How can we increase our capacity to create, test, and scale new models quickly? Although motivating an organization to change is a difficult task, it is essential in the current strategic context.

Businesses that want to use innovative business models to stimulate growth must answer several important questions: How wide should the effort's scope be? What degree of risk is appropriate to take? Does it require a continuous capability or is it a one-time exercise?

It's critical to acknowledge that not all business model innovation initiatives are created equal in order to provide answers to those queries. Executives may make wise decisions while creating the growth path by being aware of the four different methods to business model innovation:

1. **The reinventor technique** is used when a company model is gradually failing and growth prospects are unclear due to a fundamental industry problem, such as commoditization or new regulations. In order to deliver on the new improved product profitably, the organization needs to rethink its customer-value proposition and restructure its processes.

2. **The adapter approach** is used when the current core business is unlikely to withstand fundamental disruption, even with a redesign, the adapter strategy is employed. Adapters often completely leave their core business to investigate related industries or markets. In order to identify a profitable "new core" space with the best business model, adapters need to develop an innovation engine that continuously propels experimentation.

3. **The maverick approach** to grow up a possibly more successful core business, the maverick strategy uses innovative business models. Startups or rebellious established businesses are

examples of mavericks, who use their primary advantage to transform their sector and establish new benchmarks. This calls for the capacity to continuously improve the company's edge over competitors in order to spur expansion.

4. **The adventurer approach** by exploring or travelling into new or neighboring territory, the adventurer strategy rapidly grows a business's footprint. To thrive in new markets, this strategy necessitates knowing the company's competitive advantage and making calculated wagers on creative uses of it (BCG, 2022).

1.2.3 Platform-Based Enterprise Architecture

A conceptual blueprint that outlines the composition and functions of an organization is called an "enterprise architecture" (EA). Its goal is to ascertain how a business might successfully accomplish its present and future goals. Analyzing, planning, creating, and ultimately putting the findings into practice inside an organization are all part of enterprise architecture. Because EA focuses on integrating historical systems and processes to create a seamless environment, its use aids firms undergoing digital transformation.

Platform-based enterprise architecture establishes a systematic method for building and overseeing a company's technology and business operations through an integrated and organized approach. Platform-based architectures enable organizations to create flexible systems that allow for quick technological development and integration of different operational areas through their modular design and scalable foundation. The architectural framework of digital transformation enables businesses to adjust their operations for changing market conditions while using data as a fundamental resource to create value with business partners.

Enterprise architecture provides a fundamental framework which establishes the method by which enterprises will coordinate their business operations and information systems and technological framework and organizational strengths to meet their strategic goals. Organizations build their operational structure through a platform-centric digital system which functions as their primary technological foundation that organizes and manages their various capabilities. Digital platforms function as common services which provide access to their operational functions through standardized interfaces (for example application programming interfaces) while enabling real-time information sharing among internal staff members and outside business partners and customers who work together to create value.

The platform-based enterprise architecture framework extends its scope beyond technical stacks to include business structures and data frameworks and software systems and technology systems which interconnect through established integration criteria and organizational control methods. This method allows organizations to enhance their operational efficiency while they develop new business models and handle market disruptions by modifying their existing elements instead of constructing complete new systems.

The growing usage of business technologies in the 1980s led to the development of EA frameworks. They served as a means of adapting to the quick advancement of technology. Later, EA grew to include not just IT but the whole organization. The remainder of the business would then support the digital transition.

Key Features and Benefits of Platform-Based Enterprise Architecture:

- **Modularity and Reusability:** The platform architecture divides enterprise systems into reusable modular components which different business units can implement to cut development time and enhance their innovation processes.
- **Scalability and Flexibility:** Organizations can grow their capabilities through existing systems when they use scalable platform elements that include cloud services APIs and microservices instead of making extensive changes to their current infrastructure.
- **Integration and Interoperability:** The platform architecture provides standards-based integration capabilities which enable different systems to exchange data and functionality without

interruption. This system enables organizations to take advantage of real-time data to establish unified operations which enhance their decision-making capabilities.

- **Alignment with Business Strategy:** The platform-based architecture establishes basic business functions which technology should support to create alignment between IT systems and business strategies that help organizations achieve their strategic objectives such as enhancing customer experience or creating new revenue streams.
- **Support for Ecosystems and Innovation:** Digital platforms enable enterprises to establish partnerships with external organizations which include developers and customers to drive co-innovation while expanding their market presence and developing integrated value networks (Barney & Gillis, 2025).

Advantages of Enterprise Architecture

Let's examine some of the numerous advantages of enterprise architecture:

- EA insights can assist a company going through a significant transition, such a merger or digital transformation, in implementing the project more smoothly by rapidly identifying essential resources and competencies.
- By carefully evaluating existing infrastructures, enterprise architecture enables a company to spot weaknesses and inefficiencies. This draws attention to areas that could use innovation, enhancement, and optimization.
- The organization's IT assets are clearly outlined in EA documentation. System interoperability can be enhanced and complexity reduced with the use of this information. A company can cut expenses by identifying methods to get rid of redundancy and distribute resources more effectively.
- An organization can utilize data to decide which areas to prioritize when using a data-driven enterprise architecture.

Making quicker and better-informed IT investment decisions is facilitated by a greater comprehension of business capabilities.

- A company can increase communication and transparency by implementing EA since the documentation makes the infrastructure and business model easier for all departments to understand, not just IT.
- EA modelling insights can also point to measures to lower risk by enhancing information security and management and assessing the effects of such issues.
- These advantages improve an organization's operational agility and resilience, enabling it to handle shocks and stay ahead of market trends (Ardoq, 2024a).

1.3 Business and Technology Drivers

The main reasons which drive organizations to implement digital transformation methods are business needs and technological requirements. The internal operational needs of organizations together with external market pressures create the requirements which determine how urgent digital projects need to be executed and which particular areas they should focus on. The understanding of these drivers enables leaders and scholars and practitioners to create successful transformation roadmaps which match organizational capabilities to their strategic requirements.

Digital transformation extends beyond an IT project because it represents a business response to fundamental changes in operating and competitive and value creation methods. Technology advancements bring forth opportunities that improve efficiency and drive innovation and enhance user experiences while business situations require organizations to adapt to competition and customer needs and global market expansion. Companies must implement digital transformation as their main strategic goal because this process enables them to achieve sustainable growth and operational resilience and maintain market relevance during times of continuous change.

Organizations establish their core business priorities based on strategic business drivers which include market factors that determine customer experience and regulatory requirements and their ability to compete. The growth of digital technologies from cloud computing through big data analytics and artificial intelligence to the Internet of Things (IoT) enables organizations to develop new business capabilities while accessing markets which they previously could not. The two drivers of change compel organizations to develop new approaches for managing their services and production methods and their overall business operations.

Business Drivers:

- **Competitive Pressure and Market Dynamics:** Competitive pressure can be defined as the intensity of rivalry between companies in the industry and may also include the threat posed by digitally native competitors. Market dynamics involve evolving industry structures, customer behaviour and innovation cycles which force organizations to keep on changing their strategies and capabilities.
- **Customer Expectations and experience**: The customer expectations and experience are the changing needs of customers to have custom, smooth, responsive, and digital interactions among various touchpoints. This driver forces businesses to re-engineer processes and models of service delivery in order to increase satisfaction and loyalty.
- **Strategic Growth and Global Expansion Global Strategy:** The growth and international expansion are the organizational goal to expand operations, sell to markets, and diversify the revenue. Digital technologies help in expansion as geographical barriers are minimized and it also boosts distribution channels which are digital.
- **Regulatory and Compliance Requirements:** Regulatory and compliance requirements are legal, industry and governmental requirements that companies have to comply with, especially in

such aspects as data privacy, cybersecurity, financial reporting and industry-based governance structures.

- **Business Model Evolution:** The concept of business model evolution describes how a company defines, draws, and provides value. This embraces the change of traditional product-based models to digital, subscription based, platform based or service based models which are made possible through technological advancement (Cataligent, 2025).

Technology Drivers:

- **Cloud Computing:** Cloud computing refers to a technology model that provides computing resources including storage, processing power and applications on the web in a scalable and on-demand manner which makes operations flexible and cost-effective.
- **Data Analytics and Artificial Intelligence:** Data analytics is the methodical computer-assisted analysis of data to produce actionable information and Artificial Intelligence (AI) is the machine-based systems that can perform tasks that are normally done with human intelligence i.e. prediction, pattern recognition and decision making.
- **Internet of Things (IoT):** Internet of Things (IoT) is a terminology used to describe a system of interconnected physical objects with sensors, software and connection that allow real-time data exchange and automatic interaction between systems and environments.
- **Mobile and Digital Platform:** Digital interfaces Mobile and digital platforms are technology infrastructures that facilitate interaction and service delivery as well as value exchange by means of web-based digital interfaces or mobile-based digital interfaces, typically among many groups of users within an ecosystem.
- **Automation and Role in Robotic Process Automation (RPA):** Automation can be described as the application of technology in carrying out work with minimum human involvement. Robotic Process Automation (RPA) precisely deals with software bots which

are rule-based and digitized and automated processes across enterprise systems.

1.3.1 Emerging Technologies as Catalysts of Change

Emerging technologies serve as powerful catalysts of change because they transform all organizational aspects which include operational methods and competitive strategies and digital value creation methods. Emerging technologies create new operating functions which reshape existing market structures and change how businesses compete with each other. The process of digital transformation speeds up because these technologies provide organizations with innovative solutions which increase their operational performance while creating fresh business opportunities.

Organizations in the present business world implement technologies that include artificial intelligence (AI) and cloud computing and big data analytics and blockchain and Internet of Things (IoT) and advanced automation systems to transform their strategic planning and operational processes. Organizations experience more than process enhancements because these technologies create new methods for making decisions and delivering services and enabling customers to interact with businesses. The technological advancements within enterprises function as both drivers of modernization and technological advancements.

The main feature which distinguishes emerging technologies from all other technologies exists because these technologies can create disruptive innovation. The system creates new market segments by enabling startups to compete against established firms while decreasing obstacles which prevent them from entering the industry. AI-driven analytics enables organizations to make predictions about future events while cloud platforms provide enterprises with expandable systems at a low cost and IoT technology enables businesses to track their physical assets in real time. Organizations need to adopt active development pathways because these methods are forcing organizations to transform their business operations.

Organizations use emerging technologies to enhance their ability to respond to changes while creating new operational possibilities through their testing processes. Enterprises can test new concepts through cloud-native infrastructures and low-code development platforms and digital ecosystems.

Emerging technologies into the business sector at present mainly functions as essential technologies which enable companies to develop new operational models and create fresh methods for delivering value to their customers. The implementation of virtual reality technology together with other innovative systems will enable companies to achieve faster digital evolution by integrating their different operational capabilities.

- **Artificial Intelligence (AI) and Machine Learning:** Artificial Intelligence (AI) refers to computer systems which perform tasks that require human intelligence for reasoning and learning and problem-solving and decision-making. The field of Machine Learning (ML) works as a subset of artificial intelligence (AI) which enables systems to learn from data patterns and enhance their performance without needing specific programming instructions.
- **Cloud Computing:** Cloud computing delivers computing resources—including storage, processing power, and software—via the internet on a scalable, on-demand basis. The technology converts traditional IT infrastructure from its existing model of capital-intensive ownership to a contemporary service-based system.
- **Big Data and Advanced Analytics:** Big Data describes data sets which exceed traditional data management systems because of their enormous size and complex structure. Advanced analytics applies statistical methods together with predictive techniques and computational approaches to extract valuable insights from these data sets.
- **Internet of Things (IoT)**: The Internet of Things (IoT) system connects physical devices through installed sensors and

software which enable them to gather and transmit data to other devices in real time. IoT is a bridge between physical and digital spaces.

- **Blockchain Technology:** Blockchain technology functions as a distributed ledger system which enables secure transaction recording because it uses multiple nodes to achieve transparent record-keeping without needing a central authority to control its operations.
- **Robotic Process Automation (RPA):** Robotic Process Automation (RPA) enables enterprise systems to automate digital tasks through software bots which execute rules-based tasks that require repetitive execution.

1.3.2 Competitive Strategy in the Digital Economy

The concept of competitive strategy in the digital economy can be understood as the development and execution of strategic activities, which allow organizations to attain sustainable competitive advantage in digital technology-affected, data-driven innovation-based, and platform-based competitors. Digital competition is fast, connected, network effects, and constantly innovating, unlike the traditional industrial competition, which was mainly determined by the economies of scale, physical assets, and the efficiencies of the supply chain.

The digital economy is growing to rely on the capacity of an organization to use digital technologies to create customer value, maximize operations, and improve business processes. The digital platforms, data analytics, artificial intelligence, and cloud-based structures have transformed the way companies compete, collaborate, and generate value. Consequently, competitive strategy has ceased to be the process of positioning within an established industry framework; rather, it entails being a part of unstable digital ecosystems, in which companies co-create value with their partners, customers, and even competitors.

The strategic use of data is one of the characteristics of digital competition. Those organizations that can adequately gather, assess, and utilize data can make better decisions, customize customer experience, and predict market tendencies. Moreover, the digital technologies decrease barriers to entry, which means that startups and digital native companies can compete with the established ones due to innovative and flexible business models. This increases the level of competition and the need to redefine the strategic position of traditional firms.

Digital competitive strategy also focuses on:

- **Customer-Centric Value Creation:** Customer centric value creation is the strategic approach where the organizations are developing products, services and experiences with a profound knowledge of what the customers need, want and do. This in the digital economy means businesses use data analytics together with personalization technologies and digital engagement platforms to create user experiences that deliver seamless and responsive and personalized interactions across all connection points.
- **Agility and Innovation Capability**: Agility and capability of innovation is the competence of an organization to quickly respond to changes in the market, test new concepts, and constantly enhance products, processes, and business models. This is enabled in digital environments by flexible organisations, cross functional working group and iterative development process.
- **Platform Participation and Ecosystem Strategy:** Platform participation and ecosystem strategy entails use of digital platforms and collaborative networks to create value with partners, customers, and third-party developers. It is a strategic move, which builds on the interrelated digital infrastructures to increase the market reach, promote innovation, and create network effects.
- **Operational Excellence by Digitalization**: Digitalization as operational excellence is the utilization of digital technologies to streamline the business processes, make them more efficient, cost-effective, and responsive to services. This would consist of automating, analyzing and integrating enterprise systems to streamline and create real time performance monitoring.

Businesses need to combine their established competitive methods with digital transformation methods because this requirement exists as their fundamental operational need. Digital economy businesses maintain their competitive edge through two primary factors which include maintaining cost leadership and achieving differentiation together with their digital capabilities that encompass technological adaptability and their capacity to foster innovation and manage ecosystem partnerships. The process of developing competitive strategy requires organizations to approach it as an ongoing process that continuously evolves instead of treating it as a fixed method of establishing market presence.

- **Resilience and Cybersecurity:** The concept of resilience and cybersecurity is used to refer to the capacity of an organization to safeguard digital properties, the continuity of its operations, and the capability to restore to a state of normalcy in a digital environment that is linked to other interdependent digital environments. This involves the introduction of effective security measures, risk management programs and recovery programs to protect enterprise infrastructure and stake holder confidence (SwissTech Solution, 2024).

1.3.3 Regulatory, Economic, and Global Pressures

The forces which drive digital transformation and organizational strategic planning for organizations include three external factors which are regulatory requirements and economic conditions and international business trends. Modern enterprises must operate within complex institutional frameworks that emerge from three main sources which are legal systems and economic changes and international market competition and geopolitical forces. Organizations must develop adaptable operational structures and establish robust governance frameworks and digital infrastructure systems to protect their market position while staying within regulatory boundaries and safeguarding their business operations.

- **Regulatory Pressures:**

  Regulatory pressures arise from national and international laws, industry standards, and policy frameworks which govern areas of data protection and cybersecurity and financial transparency and environmental sustainability and consumer rights. The expansion of digital technologies which enable data collection and storage and processing capabilities makes regulatory compliance more essential and complicated. Governments and regulatory bodies create strict rules to protect consumer privacy while they establish ethical guidelines for AI use and digital accountability standards.

Businesses need to treat compliance as a strategic requirement because it functions beyond its traditional role as a back-office duty. Organizations need to develop digital transformation projects which will meet their current regulatory requirements while implementing secure systems and audit processes and governance structures. Noncompliance leads to financial penalties and damage to reputation and restrictions on business operations. Organizations spend money on digital risk management solutions and compliance automation systems and cybersecurity security systems to help them handle regulatory requirements.

- **Economic Pressures:**

Economic pressures originate from five factors which include market volatility and cost constraints and inflationary trends and resource scarcity and changes in consumer spending behavior. Organizations in competitive markets must continuously reduce their operational expenses while they work to improve their service delivery. Businesses can achieve cost savings through digital technologies which automate processes and integrate systems and use data to enhance operational efficiency.

Companies accelerate their digital transformation efforts during economic downturns and financial instabilities because they need to create business models that can withstand all challenges. Cloud computing enables companies to reduce their capital expenses because it delivers digital platforms which support their global operations without requiring them to construct extensive physical facilities and their analytics tools which assist with strategic decision-making. Economic pressures create driving forces which prompt organizations to implement digital innovation and operational transformation.

- **Global Pressures:**

  Globalization together with international competition and worldwide supply networks and fast-changing technological standards creates worldwide pressures which drive international business operations. Modern businesses face competition from both their home markets and international digital companies which possess greater resources and technological advantages. The competitive environment between businesses becomes more severe because of this condition which accelerates their product development efforts.

  The global interconnectedness of the world creates greater risks for organizations because it exposes them to geopolitical threats and supply chain interruptions and differences in international regulations. Organizations that want to stay competitive need to implement digital systems which work internationally and use supply chain technologies that can adapt to various situations and require digital approaches that can bridge cultural boundaries. Digital platforms and collaborative ecosystems enable enterprises to operate seamlessly across geographical boundaries while maintaining strategic coherence.

1.4 DIGITAL MATURITY AND READINESS MODELS

The ability of a company to react swiftly to technological advancements and changing trends is referred to as digital maturity. The goal is to quickly create value using these new capabilities and customer interests in order to outperform competitors. Investing in the equipment and personnel that can most effectively utilize new technologies is necessary for digital maturity.

Nearly two-thirds of manufacturing CEOs surveyed by KPMG believe that agility is the new currency of business. Being too slow will lead to our bankruptcy. One in three, however, concur that their company is finding it difficult to stay up with technology advancements.

Organizations use digital maturity and readiness models to measure their ability to adopt and implement digital transformation projects and maintain these projects over time. Digital transformation serves as the strategic goal for organizations to achieve digital capability while digital maturity shows their existing level of technological adoption and operational proficiency and cultural compatibility. Organizations demonstrate their operational ability to manage digital transformation through their current readiness to handle change.

Organizations experience challenges with enterprise modernization because they lack sufficient executive support and employee skills and appropriate governance systems and ability to adapt their workplace culture. Organizations use digital maturity and readiness models to identify their organizational gaps through systematic evaluation methods that assess various company aspects. Digital models enable businesses to evaluate their digital capabilities and decide which areas to invest in and create achievable plans for their digital transformation journey (F.Dieffenbacher, 2022).

Businesses in a variety of sectors and industries are placing a high priority on digital transformation, incorporating technology into all aspects of operations to improve customer experiences, reconfigure processes, and stay competitive in a market that is always evolving. However, different organisations have different levels of digital readiness, which can lead to adoption issues and failed transitions. In order to successfully plan, gauge success, and accomplish digital transformation objectives, organisations can use a digital transformation maturity model to evaluate and monitor digital maturity. They encourage organisations to see digital transformations as a continuous endeavor rather than a one-time alteration and offer a framework for assessing capabilities.

A maturity model is an organized framework that companies use, frequently in a phased manner, to evaluate the skills of their team in a particular area of concentration. A digital transformation maturity model aids organisations in evaluating and comprehending their present level of digital readiness, pinpointing opportunities for development, and monitoring their advancement toward greater levels of digital maturity.

Since effective transformation is about mentality and tools, a maturity model in digital transformation assesses not only technology but also people, processes, and culture. Change management for digital transformation, or a combined emphasis on the technical and human aspects of change, is therefore crucial (Prosci, 2025).

Digital Maturity Model

Models of digital transformation maturity vary. Some concentrate on specific company divisions, such as sales or marketing. Others concentrate on certain skills like data management, creativity, or artificial intelligence. To put it briefly, DMMs provide data-driven insights about the progress of the digital transformation process. This aids in deciding the next course of action. Businesses go through five different stages as they transition from traditional to completely digital organisations, according to the Digital Maturity Model. These phases consist of:

- **Ad-Hoc**: At this point, companies are reactive rather than proactive. It's possible that their digital initiatives were non-existent or simply dispersed. Although their team may be utilizing very basic digital tools, the organization does not appear to have a defined plan.
- **Opportunistic:** Businesses begin experimenting with their digital solutions at this point. There is some awareness of the possibilities of new digital technologies, even though their team may start with isolated projects. However, the adoption of these technologies won't be consistent.
- **Managed:** The third phase will see increased coordination of digital transformation initiatives. Organisations may begin to invest in digital technologies that are scalable. Additionally, they will create cross-departmental projects. It is evident that digital strategy and corporate goals are in line.

- **Optimized:** A lot of information about the business environment is reflected at this stage. Businesses in the stage have a digital transformation strategy that is quantifiable and well-defined. Decision-making based on data is prioritized. Additionally, daily company activities make advantage of digital procedures.
- **Innovative:** Businesses attain the pinnacle of digital maturity in this final level. Their long-term strategic goals are fueled by their constant innovation and digital transformation. They frequently make use of cutting-edge technology like predictive analytics, AI, and machine learning. These technologies are employed to improve operational excellence and elevate client experiences (DynaTech Systems, 2024).

Readiness Models

The Digital Maturity Models (DMMs) use readiness models as additional support because these models assess an organization's ability to execute and control digital transformation from its current digital development phase. Readiness models evaluate organizational readiness while maturity models measure organizational progress at a specific point in time.

Digital readiness focuses on the essential structural elements, cultural aspects, strategic elements, and technological requirements which organizations must establish to succeed in their transformation efforts. Organizations may recognize the importance of digital change but without leadership commitment together with workforce capabilities and governance structures and resource allocation, their transformation efforts will remain incomplete. Organizations use readiness models as diagnostic tools which help them detect internal deficiencies before starting major digital transformation projects.

The significance of the Prime Directive, or the company's corporate vision, is also recognized by an organization using the Operational Excellence Enterprise Readiness Model. All components of a business can make sure they are working toward the same objectives by coordinating any operational excellence initiatives with this vision: to look for new products, new markets, and odd new business prospects (Boer, 2022).

1.4.1 Digital Maturity Models and Assessment Frameworks

An organization's thorough adoption of the digital transformation process is referred to as digital maturity. representing the current state of a business's digital transformation and offering information on the accomplishments of that business's transformation initiatives. The concept requires complete organizational alignment with digital age operations because it requires more than only using technological solutions. The company has achieved complete system integration because its internal processes and customer interactions operate through optimized systems that support creative work and efficient production. Organizations with digital maturity are defined by their ability to use technology while they adapt to market changes and pursue new opportunities and create a culture that supports ongoing progress in digital transformation. The concept of digital maturity describes three different development levels which organizations must follow from basic digital adoption to their final goal of achieving strategic innovation.

Digital Maturity Models

A digital maturity model establishes a framework which organizations follow to achieve their strategic and technological development. The system provides organizations with a structured framework which guides them through the stages of innovation their development process and their technology implementation. The models provide organizations with two essential elements which include a defined advancement path and a structured system to determine their current digital maturity status. Organizations use digital maturity models to assess their digital capabilities through three key areas which include their technological abilities and operational processes and organizational culture. The models provide firms with two essential benefits which include the ability to build customized methods for digital competency improvement and the ability to evaluate their digital development progress.

Digital Maturity Assessments

The digital maturity assessment process applies a systematic assessment method to determine an organization's current digital maturity level through its digital maturity model system. The assessment process involves studying the organization's operational processes, its cultural environment, how it adopts new technologies, and how its strategies match its objectives. The assessment process will evaluate the organization's digital abilities through two methods which will help identify its main strengths and weaknesses. A digital maturity assessment enables organizations to gain valuable insights about their current technological capabilities and strategic business direction and their potential to drive innovation. The company uses these insights to make informed decisions that help them determine project priorities and improve their digital strategy and create achievable progress targets. A digital maturity assessment enables organizations to evaluate their current digital status while providing them with a framework to develop their future digital capabilities in a world that constantly evolves.

Digital maturity represents the highest stage of digital development which organizations achieve. The process requires complete organizational transformation which includes digital technology implementation throughout all aspects of business operations and organizational culture development. Organizations at this level have reached the necessary expertise to utilize technology as a tool for driving both creative development and operational improvements.

The digital maturity models serve as the essential basis which supports this entire transformation process. The established frameworks show an organization which begins its digital transformation journey to its ultimate strategic management achievements through the different digital transformation stages which it will experience. The models provide guidance as organisations go through various phases, allowing them to assess their progress and strategically plan their course. Digital Maturity Assessments complete this active three-part system which transforms theoretical knowledge into practical advancements. The assessments examine an organization's digital capabilities through a selected model framework, which produces specific insights about its strengths, weaknesses, and areas of potential development. Companies use these insights to modify their strategies because they enable them to reach digital maturity through informed decision-making and optimized processes. (Solution, 2023).

1.4.2 Leadership, Governance, and Digital Culture

Digital transformation projects may rise or fall depending on three core tenets: leadership, governance and digital culture. The implementation of digital transformation projects depends on technology as a resource but their successful execution depends on three factors which include leadership direction and governance discipline and organizational culture. Digital transformation represents more than a technical transition because it requires organizations to implement strategic and cultural transformations which need complete institutional backing.

Digital Leadership as a Strategic Necessity

Digital leadership requires organizations to use digital technology for their operational needs. The process requires leaders to develop future-oriented strategies together with their expertise in technological systems and their skills to manage organizational changes. The leaders who guide organizations through digital transformation need to develop a digital vision which combines their present digital capabilities with their future business goals. The organization will use this vision to identify its technology needs while determining the digital capabilities which will create value for customers and drive operational improvements.

Digital leaders in organizations show two main abilities which help them adapt to new situations. The digital economy creates an environment where customer needs keep changing and businesses need to react to sudden technological advancements. Leaders need to establish an environment which allows people to conduct experiments while they develop new ideas through their work with ongoing development activities. The team needs to decide how to distribute their resources which includes choosing which digital projects to fund while they work on making digital changes that will affect all organizational divisions instead of just the IT department.

Digital Accountability Governance Frameworks

Governance functions as the essential element which transforms digital objectives into concrete measurable results. Digital governance describes the established rules and procedures together with their accountability systems which direct digital projects to achieve corporate objectives and adhere to legal standards and ethical guidelines. The absence of governance leads to digital transformation challenges which result in organizational priorities becoming disjointed and uncoordinated and unfocused execution of digital transformation initiatives.

Digital initiatives need to deliver measurable value through their implementation because governance functions as a safeguard against technology experiments becoming unproductive. The system distributes resources openly to its users while maintaining performance evaluation processes as their accountable assessment method. Digital systems in regulated industries must establish governance frameworks that incorporate compliance requirements and data protection standards into their architectural design.

Digital Culture as the Main Force for Sustaining Progress

The leadership establishes organizational direction while governance systems create structural frameworks which digital culture maintains ongoing transformation initiatives. Digital culture defines the organizational values which employees share together with their beliefs and behavior patterns that enable them to create new ideas and work together and acquire knowledge through data analysis. The system demonstrates how workers understand digital transformation and use technological systems throughout their workday.

An organization establishes a powerful digital culture through its willingness to test new ideas and its capacity to handle calculated risks and its commitment to ongoing education. Employees need the freedom to challenge existing methods and bring forward new ideas while using digital resources to boost their work results. Organizations that maintain strict hierarchical structures together with a mindset that avoids risks face difficulties when they try to execute digital projects successfully.

The digital culture of an organization supports teams from different departments to work together. Digital transformation requires marketing teams to collaborate with IT specialists while data analysts work together with operations managers and their leadership teams use direct engagement to drive technological innovation processes. The organization benefits from its collaborative culture because it enhances knowledge exchange which leads to faster progress in transformation.

The three elements of leadership and governance and digital culture form an interconnected system. The strategic direction of an organization gets defined by leadership, while governance establishes a framework for implementation, and organizational culture shapes the everyday conduct of employees. The digital transformation process gets disrupted when any of these three elements experiences a weakness. The absence of governance results in organizations facing difficulties because they lack the ability to turn their visionary concepts into practical operations, while organizations that have governance but lack cultural backing experience compliance-driven transformations that yield minimal innovation results.

Digital transformation requires organizations to change through their complete business operations and their technological systems. The combination of leadership and digital culture enables organizations to build their governance systems which maintain operational discipline. Companies that successfully integrate these three elements will create a sustainable base that supports their digital innovation efforts and their ability to gain market advantages and their strategic expansion in the digital business world.

1.4.3 Change Management and Transformation Readiness

Digital transformation does not represent a technological modernization; it is first of all an organizational change process which redefines structures, workflows, occupational roles, and cultural practices. Thus, change management and transformation preparedness become the keys to success. Although digital maturity models evaluate the ability of technology, transformation readiness determines the ability of an organization to take in and hold on to change by evaluating its behavioural, structural and strategic capacity.

Change management as applied to digital transformation is a methodical way to prepare, equip, and support people and groups in embracing new technologies, processes and business models. It entails matching the organizational goals with the engagement of the employees, leadership dedication, and communication approaches. Devoid of formal change management processes, even the well-invested digital projects are prone to opposition, misalignment, and ultimate failure.

Transformation readiness, in its turn, indicates the willingness of the organization to implement, as well as continue with digital change. It involves a variety of dimensions:

- **Leadership Commitment and Vision Clarity:** Effective transformation requires executive endorsement to achieve successful results. Leaders must provide a complete digital vision together with their strategic goals and they need to demonstrate their ability to adapt. Their commitment serves as a signal that the organization considers this matter to be its top priority which helps to decrease uncertainty.
- **Cultural Adaptability and Learning Orientation:** An organization becomes digitally ready when it establishes a work environment that supports experimental work and ongoing educational activities and permits employees to take measured risks. Organizations that operate with strict hierarchical structures and isolated departments face difficulties when attempting to implement agile and platform-based operational systems.
- **Capability and Skill Readiness:** The organization requires three essential skills which include digital literacy for the workforce and cross-functional collaboration abilities and data-driven decision-making skills. The organization needs to develop its readiness through two actions which include hiring new staff members and training current employees for their existing roles.

- **Structural and Process Flexibility:** The quick development of new ideas faces obstacles from established governance systems and their accompanying bureaucratic practices. The organizations need to assess their current structures to determine if they enable agile development and cross-departmental collaboration and quick prototype testing.
- **Stakeholder Alignment and Communication:** The organization needs to implement clear communication methods because they help employees understand the goals and advantages and forecast results of transformation initiatives.

Organizations require continuous change management capabilities which should not be considered short-term solutions. Digital transformation processes require ongoing development which interacts with three factors: technological progress, market trends, and regulatory requirements. Organizations must conduct periodic evaluations to assess their readiness because their preparation needs to be updated.

1.5 TRANSFORMATION STRATEGY AND ROADMAPS

Organizations use their transformation strategy and roadmaps as their primary method to change their digital goals into tangible operational work. The digital transformation process requires organizations to develop a detailed plan of action which they will execute through successive stages to achieve their strategic goals. The absence of a complete transformation framework results in digital projects for organizations which face their primary business challenges through uncontrolled development and insufficient alignment with their organizational objectives.

The transformation strategy establishes the complete vision and objectives which direct the organization's digital development path. The document explains the reasons for transformation and the expected benefits it will bring and the ways digital resources will strengthen market competitiveness. Organizations use this strategy to connect their digital projects with their main business objectives which results in technology spending that directly drives value creation and better operational processes and improved customer service and sustained business development.

The elements of a transformation strategy comprise multiple components which include the following

- **Strategic Vision and Objectives** – The organization needs to define its digital goals which will support both its corporate mission and its future growth objectives.
- **Value Proposition Redesign** – The project will discover the ways that digital technologies will transform all aspects of their product and service offerings and their customer interaction methods.
- **Capability Development Plans** – The development plans focus on building two main areas which include technology infrastructure and data management systems together with digital skills and innovation process development.
- **Governance and Leadership Alignment** – The process establishes systems for responsibility assignment and executive control of operations.
- **Performance Metrics and KPIs** – Measurable indicators to evaluate progress and transformation impact.

The transformation roadmap shows organizations how to implement their strategic goals. The digital initiatives roadmap shows all activities which need to be completed and when those activities will happen and which activities depend on others. The document functions as an operational guide which helps organizations distribute resources while controlling risks and handling changes.

Key elements of a transformation roadmap include:

- **Current-State Assessment:** Current-state assessment of an organization requires systematic evaluation of its current digital systems and technology infrastructure and operational processes and employee competencies and organizational culture to assess its digital maturity level and determine its existing capability deficiencies.

- **Prioritization of Initiatives:** Prioritization of initiatives acts as a strategic procedure which enables organizations to identify and rank digital transformation projects according to their possible effects and execution difficulty and needs for resources and their match with business objectives.
- **Phased Implementation Plan:** A phased implementation plan establishes a structured framework which divides digital transformation work into multiple stages that progress from basic development to advanced digital capabilities.
- **Resource Allocation and Budget Planning:** The process of resource allocation together with budget planning allows organizations to allocate their financial resources and technological resources and their workforce to complete their digital transformation projects.
- **Risk Mitigation and Contingency Planning:** Organizations use risk mitigation and contingency planning to identify and assess potential operational and technological and cybersecurity and regulatory and organizational risks which arise during their digital transformation process.

Organizations develop their transformation roadmaps through incremental methods instead of executing complete organizational transformations through one-time projects. Organizations can use agile methodologies together with modular implementation methods to develop solutions which they will test until they reach their desired outcomes. The iterative model enables organizations to protect themselves from risks while developing their ability to adjust to changes which occur within digital environments.

Successful transformation strategies need to achieve complete integration between different business departments. Digital transformation affects marketing operations together with finance systems and supply chain management and human resources operations. Organizations need to establish cross-departmental collaboration because it helps them prevent operational silos which would harm their ability to operate as a unified business.

The implementation of change management stands as a fundamental element which organizations use to develop their transformation strategies. Organizations must develop new cultural standards which require employees to follow new workflows while acquiring new competencies to implement digital initiatives. The development of successful roadmaps requires organizations to create communication strategies which include training initiatives and methods for engaging stakeholders and systems for tracking performance to handle resistance while maintaining project progress (Pitliya, 2025).

1.5.1 Vision Formulation and Strategic Alignment

The current digital environment requires organizations to establish their strategic vision while maintaining complete alignment between their digital initiatives and business objectives to achieve successful transformation initiatives. The development of a vision combined with strategic alignment establishes the complete transformation roadmap development process. The organizational change process requires these elements to establish the path forward and maintain operational consistency throughout the organization.

Vision Formulation in the Digital Era

Organizations use vision formulation as a formal process to determine their future goals for operating in a digital environment. A digital vision describes more than an organization implementing new technologies because it outlines the complete value creation pathway and marketplace competition strategy and long-term growth plan of the organization.

Strategic Alignment as an Integrative Mechanism

Strategic Alignment serves as a mechanism that brings different elements together. The vision establishes direction for the organization while strategic alignment maintains organizational consistency. The process of strategic alignment connects all digital transformation goals with the complete corporate strategy. The system guarantees that all technological spending and process changes and organizational development activities will directly advance overall business objectives.

The process of alignment happens through different alignment dimensions:

- **Corporate-Level Alignment** – Digital initiatives must reinforce long-term corporate strategy, competitive positioning, and value propositions.
- **Functional-Level Alignment** – The departments of operations, marketing, finance, and human resources must work together on digital initiatives to avoid operational disruptions.
- **Technological Alignment** - Digital systems and IT infrastructure must provide active support for strategic objectives instead of functioning as separate technical systems.

The absence of alignment causes digital projects to become separate initiatives which do not produce any measurable results. A substantial IT matter that fosters cost efficiency, strategic alignment is the one cachet that aligns resources in a way that the business will see returns on its investment.

Leadership and Communication in Alignment

The execution of organizational vision depends on leaders who establish the connection between vision and execution. Senior executives must champion the digital vision through their active communication of its importance which they should integrate into all strategic planning activities. Transparent communication decreases doubt which helps people accept organizational changes while improving their dedication to the company.

The company needs to establish measurable objectives which will function as performance indicators to assess how digital projects align with its strategic objectives. This process allows organizations to continuously assess and enhance their transformation initiatives.

The Strategic Importance of Transformation Roadmaps

The transformation strategy requires vision formulation to establish the end goal while strategic alignment directs all activities toward that goal. The two elements together enable organizations to transform their digital goals into organized operational plans.

Organizations that prioritize this foundational stage are more likely to experience coherent implementation sustainable digital maturity and long-term competitive resilience. The absence of vision clarity and alignment results in organizations making uncoordinated financial commitments which lead to unpredictable results.

The digital transformation process needs its foundation to be established through vision formulation and strategic alignment. The transformation process needs purposefulness and coordinated efforts and strategic guidance to help organizations successfully deal with digital economic challenges (CATALYST, 2016).

1.5.2 Enterprise-Wide Transformation Planning

Enterprise-wide transformation planning is the methodology that provides an organization with the capability to articulate digital vision into integrated action by all business functions. Enterprise-wide planning on the other hand is more holistic and strategically aligned and institutionalized unlike isolated digital efforts that are limited to IT departments or specific operational units.

Digital transformation influences all the aspects of the organization such as strategy, operations, customer engagement, supply chains, governance structures, and organizational culture. Thus, enterprise-wide planning involves cross functional integration to harmonize a business strategy, technology architecture, data management and human capital development in a single roadmap.

In essence, enterprise-wide transformation planning entails a number of essential elements:

- **Strategic Alignment Cross-Functional:** Change efforts should be directly reported to corporate goals. There should be a common understanding of digital priorities between the business units, IT departments, finance, operations, and human resources. Alignment eliminates overlap, fragmentation of investments and reinforces organizational coherence.

- **Integrated Business and Technology Roadmap**: This is a detailed plan of how to implement the system in phases, develop capabilities, upgrade the system, as well as the innovation milestones. The roadmap will help create the linkage between long-range strategic aspirations and short-range operational deliverables so that the transformation will proceed in viable and quantifiable phases.
- **Cross-Functional Governance Structures**: To have good planning, there must be governance structures that lead to coordination of decisions made by the departments. Steering committees, transformation offices, and digital leadership councils are useful in creating accountability and risk management as well as prioritization of resources at enterprise level.
- **Resource Synchronization and Capability Building**: Enterprise-wide planning has to consider financial investment, technological infrastructure, workforce skills, and organizational capacity. There should be synchronization of the budget allocation, talent development and technology acquisition strategies to avoid implementation bottlenecks.
- **Change Integration and Stakeholder Engagement**: Transformation will impact a combination of employees, partners and customers, so careful planning should include organized communication and engagement systems. This requires organization-wide implementation through lessening opposition and promoting cooperation between ranks.

Notably, the planning of transformation of enterprises across the board is not a document but a dynamic strategy. The digital environment is rapidly changing because of technological advancement, regulatory changes and competition. In that way, the planning structures should be dynamic, including the constant monitoring, feedback mechanisms, and strategic refocusing.

1.5.3 Performance Monitoring and Strategic Control

The organization uses performance monitoring together with strategic control to assess and correct digital transformation projects which need to maintain their progress toward business goals. The transformation strategies establish the overall direction and scope of the project whereas performance monitoring shows actual results to check if the team achieves its defined project goals. The leadership team uses strategic control to make operational changes and shift resources and adjust their primary focuses based on internal assessments and external environmental shifts.

Digital transformation requires new performance assessment methods because conventional measurement systems fail to meet its needs. Digital projects require organizations to work through multiple development cycles which require technological advancements and cross-departmental teamwork. The monitoring system needs to track financial results together with non-financial metrics which show how technology gets used and how efficient processes run and how customers interact and how innovation potential develops and how cultural transformation happens.

Several factors contribute to an effective monitoring:

- **Key Performance Indicators (KPIs) and Digital Metrics:** Organizations have to be able to establish measurable indicators, which correspond to strategic objectives. They can be measures like system integration rates, digital adoption rates, the effectiveness of process automation, customer satisfaction rates, platform scalability and data utilization effectiveness. Well indicated KPIs are transparent and accountable.
- **Balanced Measurement Structures**: The performance review must incorporate financial performance with operational, customer, innovation and learning outlooks. Such a moderate practice will guarantee that it is not short-run profitability that will make the long-term capability building and strategic renewal focal.

- **Real-Time Analytics and Dashboards:** Digital transformation allows constant data gathering by the means of enterprise systems and analytics platforms. Proactive decision making can be made by use of real-time dashboards, which enable leaders to realize deviations, performance bottlenecks, and new risks at an early stage.
- **Feedback Loops (Strategic):** There needs to be the monitoring mechanisms that have a direct connection to governance and decision-making structures. Feedback loops make it possible to refine strategies iteratively to make transformation initiatives flexible and responsive to shifts in market and technology.
- **Risk and Compliance Oversight:** Strategic control is also about the regulation of compliance with regulations, cybersecurity threats, and service vulnerabilities. There is more exposure to data breaches, system failures and legal complexities in digital environments and therefore oversight is an essential aspect of performance governance.

Notably, performance monitoring in digital transformation does not only concern control but also learning. The situation where the organizations consider performance data as strategic asset encourages the continuous improvement and innovation. With the integration of monitoring systems as part of enterprise architecture and governance systems, companies establish information transparency, accountability, and flexibility.

1.6 LEGACY SYSTEMS AND MODERNIZATION NEEDS

An organization's strategic endeavor to revitalize its legacy software applications and systems is known as legacy modernization. Aligning these technologies with the latest industry standards and changing business requirements requires this procedure. Although these antiquated systems frequently continue to function, operational efficiency and creativity may be hampered by their antiquated architecture, dependence on antiquated technologies, and challenges integrating with contemporary solutions.

Legacy systems don't always need to be replaced in order to be modernized. The process requires multiple approaches which enable organizations to optimize their existing resources while they work to improve system functionality and system performance and system security and system maintainability. Organizations can select from different modernization approaches which vary in their operational impact and implementation difficulty. The organization can choose between two categories of tactics which include less invasive solutions and complete system transformation methods. Organizations use hybrid approaches to meet specific needs and operational constraints because they help manage multiple methods.

Established companies demonstrate their operational methods through their use of legacy systems which consist of software, hardware, and processes that organizations have used for many years. The systems support essential business operations which companies have built up throughout their history of operation. The systems start to limit organizations because their customer needs and market conditions and technological developments change. Organizations need to modernize because they must identify the differences between their existing legacy systems and their future operational requirements.

Why legacy systems matter in the digital era

- **Operational dependence vs. strategic mismatch:** Legacy systems maintain critical business functions but their current operational design hinders achievement of modern company objectives and market demands. The systems provide dependable performance for daily operations but they cannot handle digital service delivery or platform unification or data-based decision-making.
- **Hidden cost of maintenance and technical debt:** Running outdated systems requires organizations to spend excessive amounts of money and staff resources. Organizations face operational risks because of technical debt and they lack sufficient maintenance staff and their systems cannot work with modern technologies.

- **Impediment to agility and rapid innovation:** Organizations face obstacles to conducting fast experiments and delivering smooth customer journeys and joining digital business networks because of their unchanging technology frameworks and separated data storage and their extensive coding systems. Organizations with legacy systems experience slowed operational changes which prevents them from taking advantage of fresh market possibilities and upcoming regulatory requirements.

Modernization needs

Modernization requires three fundamental needs for its implementation. The process of modernization requires organizations to replace their outdated software systems while they should conduct a complete transformation of their technological infrastructure and organizational structure to achieve their planned strategic changes. The following needs typically drive modernization efforts:

The following needs typically drive modernization efforts:

- **Alignment with business capabilities and value creation:** Business priorities should control modernization processes because technology needs should not define modernization development. Modernization projects create valuable results when organizations map their existing systems to the business functions those systems enable. The Thought Works guidance demonstrates that organizations need to measure their progress through capability development because this method shows actual business results and builds continuous support from their operational departments.
- **Selective modernization, not blanket migration:** The process of modernizing systems requires organizations to implement selective upgrades instead of performing complete system migrations. An organization needs to assess its outdated systems to determine which elements require equal treatment and which elements need special

handling. The process of modernization involves organizations determining their essential business functions which they will develop first while they discontinue their obsolete assets and use their standardized systems to deliver shared services. The implementation of this modernizing discipline enables organizations to complete their work more effectively while protecting their business interests.

- **The development of capability-driven architecture and platform systems:** The process of modernization enables organizations to replace their existing systems with modular systems that use platform-based architectural designs. Organizations can develop a contemporary service and data platform through capability and sub-capability mapping which enables them to eliminate duplicate elements and speed up their upcoming development processes.
- **Managing complexity, risk, and change**: Legacy systems operate through complex dependencies which create data incompatibilities and protect established organizational procedures. Organizations need structured governance and risk management systems together with gradual implementation methods to achieve their modernization objectives while maintaining operational security. The objective of this project maintains operational continuity while transforming systems to achieve their modernized state (Bhattacharjee, 2025).

1.6.1 Modernization Pathways and Migration Strategies

Organizations need to modernize their existing systems because this process requires multiple steps instead of using one technical solution. The organizations use this section to select their migration strategies which include different pathways from their existing fixed systems to their upcoming digital platforms which enable them to achieve their ongoing digital transformation goals.

A pathway serves as the foundation for organizations to create their future development plans. The system between existing systems and upcoming technology implementation needs to be maintained because of its practical business benefits. The approach leads to positive outcomes because organizations will achieve their modernization targets when they create their business objectives. Practitioners note that many organizations invest heavily in modernization yet fail to realize expected outcomes when initiatives lack a holistic view of business context, capability, and governance. Thought Works' analysis of modernization efforts shows that organizations need to establish proper alignment before they will spend their resources into building complete systems which deliver their needed value.

The established pathway defines the objective of the organization because it identifies necessary changes to operational abilities and critical systems and the target future state of the organization. The organization needs this information to ensure that its modernization activities achieve strategic goals while providing competitive benefits and safeguarding technical equipment.

Common migration strategy options:

The various frameworks define different terms yet the practical guidance which they provide shows multiple common migration strategies. The three options bring different results because they affect operational needs and potential hazards and capacity to adapt over time:

- **Rehost or lift-and-shift:** The strategy enables organizations to move their current applications into a new environment which often uses cloud infrastructure without needing to change their existing code. The method allows fast execution while decreasing operational limitations. The method needs further development to achieve better interface capabilities.
- **Refactor or re-architect**: The current systems will gain improved system design through the implementation of microservices and APIs and containerization technology. The process of refactoring extends the useful life of outdated assets while preparing systems for both current platform integration needs and upcoming technological advances.

- **Rebuild or rewrite:** The organization will create a new application which uses modern architectural systems to replace its outdated legacy system. The system allows users to utilize present-day technologies and design standards. The system needs organizations to allocate substantial resources while maintaining oversight over its implementation and monitoring potential hazards. Organizations should use this solution when their business assets require essential investments.
- **Replace with packaged or platform solutions:** The organization will use both pre-built products and platform-based solutions to handle specific operational needs. The solution enables faster delivery for operational needs. The solution needs organizations to align their business operations with their training programs and organizational changes because these factors impact system adoption and value creation.
- **Retain or retire**: Organizations will keep certain legacy elements preserved in their original form until the designated time period concludes or they will remove these elements from their operations when their strategic importance decreases. The organization saves money through its plan to discontinue specific computer systems. The organization intends to allocate its resources toward essential system enhancements.

Data migration refers to the method which transfers data between different systems and formats and storage locations during times of infrastructure changes between cloud migrations and system upgrades. The transfer process needs detailed planning together with mapping and validation procedures to protect data during its movement between systems. The procedure requires multiple types of migration which include storage and application and cloud migration together with the need to move databases and applications and complete data centers. The successful transfer of data enables businesses to access critical information in their new environment which leads to reduced system downtime while protecting data from loss and ensuring uninterrupted business operations.

Enterprises use hybrid strategies to implement different system solutions across their business units and various time periods. The mission-critical system requires immediate refactoring work while the less critical system will undergo retirement or replacement at a future time. The selected combination system of the three elements shows how urgent business needs and available technology and planned system development will determine future system architecture (Mitchell, 2025).

1.6.2 Structural Limitations of Legacy IT Systems

The technological foundation of many old-established businesses is legacy IT, which has been used to run such mission critical functions as finance, supply chain management, and customer databases. But although these systems have traditionally guaranteed operational stability, they tend to pose serious structural constraints in the digital transformation scenario. Traditional architecture was built in previous technological conditions and is generally not that flexible, scalable and interoperable as needed in new platform-based digital ecosystems.

Architectural rigidity is one of the major structural constraints of legacy systems. Most traditional systems are constructed using monolithic architecture whereby the parts are closely integrated and inter-dependent. This architecture complicates and is very expensive with a modification process because even trivial changes may impact various modules that are interdependent. This leads to a slowdown in the innovation cycles and organizations fail to react fast to the changing market demands.

The other weakness is that it has limited scalability and performance issues. Old infrastructures used to be built to support predictable load in controlled environments. Conversely, modern digital businesses have to deal with dynamic and high-volume data stream and real-time transactions. Old systems might not be elasticly scalable, which prevents the organization to grow its operations or add the new digital services effectively.

The structure barrier is also a major issue of integration. Most legacy platforms were not created based on open standards or API connectivity. This poses challenges to integration with cloud platform, third-party applications, mobile applications, and new technologies like artificial intelligence or advanced analytics. As a result, businesses might have data silos, broken workflows, and a decreased level of interoperability between business units.

Also, there is a high likelihood that legacy systems use old-fashioned programming languages and technologies. These systems are expensive to maintain because of the lack of qualified practitioners that would help in their maintenance, which adds to the operational risk as well as long term maintenance expenses. This volume of obsolete parts over time leads to technical debt which causes resources to go towards maintaining the system than towards innovation.

Structural limitations are also suggested by security vulnerabilities. Advanced architectures are likely to be vulnerable to breaches, data leakage, and compliance risks because older architectures do not follow current standards of cybersecurity. In more controlled online spaces, these weaknesses can present organizations with legal liabilities and reputational harm. These obstacles notwithstanding, legacy systems should not be considered as barriers only. They are good sources of knowledge within an organization and historical information. Nevertheless, they are limited structurally, which demands modernization policies, which can manage the risk and still be innovative. Businesses should critically consider refactor, re-platform, or slow replacement of old parts as a subset of a wider set of digital transformation needs.

1.6.3 Technical Debt and Organizational Constraints

Technical debt is the total cost of technology choices in the past that were taken to create short-term efficiency or quick deployment but led to long-term complexity, increased maintenance, and decreased system flexibility. Technical debt is one of the most important modernizing barriers in the framework of digital transformation. It is a result of old software architecture, redundant systems, poorly documented code, temporary fixes and fissured integration layers that have grown over time.

Change organizations grow and make adaptations to the variable needs of the business; incremental additions in technology usually take place without any deliberate architectural plan. These short-term fixes, though only initially convenient, bury complex layers that inhibit agility and innovation. The expenses of supporting the old systems, fixing security loopholes, and assimilating systems that do not work with others rise significantly with time. Funds that should be used to innovate and develop strategic digital projects are used in the maintenance of the system and stabilization of its operations.

Technical debt is not purely a technological problem, but it is closely connected with organizational limitations. Disjointed IT and business strategies are often caused by structural silos in enterprises. Where there is independent technology decision making across the departments, the systems become disjointed and are not interoperable. This disintegration makes the combination of data complex, hampers cross-functional co-operation and limits visibility on an enterprise level.

Technical debt can also be increased by organizational culture. The lack of risk-averse leadership, change resistance, and low levels of digital literacy might prevent active modernization. Rather than making an investment in architectural redesign or modernization, companies can instead keep adding temporary solutions to old systems. This reactive strategy exposes more risk over the long-term and restricts the adoption of new technology in the organization, including cloud computing, artificial intelligence, or sophisticated analytics.

Budgetary constraints also have a big role to play. The modernization projects are usually very expensive financially and could interfere with the immediate working performance. Consequently, organizations can delay all the required upgrades, letting technical debt build up. In the long run, this becomes a vicious cycle whereby the maintenance expenditure is absorbing a greater proportion of IT budgets further limiting strategic innovation.

Technical debt is a problem that has to be resolved in a well-organized and strategic manner. The organizations should undertake regular evaluations of old systems; modernization should be prioritized on the basis of business impact and technical debt minimization should be compulsory in the transformation planning of the enterprise. It requires governance mechanisms, architectural standards and cross functional coordination to ensure that additional debt is not collected and system flexibility and scalability are slowly improved.

1.7 SUMMARY

The chapter determines that digital transformation functions as a strategic transformation which extends beyond ordinary technological updates. It traces how enterprises evolved from early data processing and integrated systems toward platform-driven, data-intensive operations, and it clarifies key concepts which separate digitization from digitalization and complete digital transformation. The chapter demonstrates that transformation needs both social and technical elements to succeed because organizations must synchronize their technological systems with their employee base and cultural values and their leadership structure and their governance systems and their outside forces. The research demonstrates that platform-based architectural system, new business models, and emerging technologies enable organizations to expand their operational capacities because they create new possibilities which lead to increased business opportunities. Organizations need structured maturity assessments and readiness evaluations and effective leadership and proper governance and organizational support systems to deal with complicated situations. The chapter demonstrates that organizations must treat their existing systems as essential resources which create difficulties for their operations, because they must modernize these systems while navigating dangerous situations. The research shows that organizations face major difficulties with modernization because they need to execute extensive business transformations which require their front-line employees to work together while their modernization efforts stay incomplete. The chapter establishes that organizations need to establish their digital goals through clear vision development, which must lead to strategic alignment and phased modernization pathways and integrated governance systems, to maintain their competitive edge throughout the digital economy.

Multiple Choice Questions (MCQs)

1. **What is the primary goal of digital transformation?**
   A. Reducing workforce size
   B. Enhancing business processes using digital technologies
   C. Eliminating all legacy systems
   D. Increasing manual processes
2. **Which of the following best defines digital transformation?**
   A. Adoption of a single new technology
   B. Complete automation of business processes
   C. Integration of digital technology into all business areas
   D. Replacement of employees with machines
3. **Which is NOT a typical driver of digital transformation?**
   A. Changing customer expectations
   B. Competitive market pressures
   C. Decreasing data availability
   D. Technological advancements
4. **What does a digital maturity model help organizations assess?**
   A. Employee salaries
   B. Level of digital adoption and capability
   C. Hardware inventory
   D. Office infrastructure
5. **Which stage typically represents the highest level of digital maturity?**
   A. Initial
   B. Developing
   C. Optimized
   D. Ad hoc

6. **What is the purpose of a digital transformation roadmap?**

   A. To track employee attendance

   B. To define step-by-step implementation of transformation initiatives

   C. To replace business strategy

   D. To manage financial audits

7. **Which of the following is a common challenge with legacy systems?**

   A. High scalability

   B. Easy integration with modern platforms

   C. High maintenance costs and limited flexibility

   D. Low operational risk

8. **Which technology is commonly associated with digital transformation?**

   A. Typewriters

   B. Cloud computing

   C. Fax machines

   D. Manual ledgers

9. **What is a key component of a successful transformation strategy?**

   A. Ignoring customer needs

   B. Clear vision and leadership alignment

   C. Avoiding change management

   D. Limiting technology adoption

10. **Why is modernization of legacy systems important?**
    A. To increase manual workload
    B. To reduce innovation
    C. To improve agility, scalability, and integration
    D. To eliminate all existing data

Answers

1	2	3	4	5	6	7	8	9	10
B	C	C	B	C	B	C	B	B	C

Chapter 2

Enterprise Architecture and Platform Modernization

1.1 OVERVIEW

The essential framework of Enterprise Architecture (EA) serves as the fundamental structure which organizations use to design and execute their digital transformation initiatives. Organizations require architectural systems to create structured pathways which connect their strategic business objectives with their technology implementations during periods of market instability and technological changes and customer behavior shifts. The system specifies all components which include business capabilities and applications and data assets and infrastructure elements that work together to generate sustainable value. The absence of an effective architectural system leads to multiple execution problems because digital projects experience system duplication issues and face challenges with system integration and security vulnerabilities and increasing technical debt. Enterprise architecture functions as more than just a documentation task because it serves as a vital organizational capability that guarantees that all modernization projects will result in systems that can collaborate and operate in future environments.

Exploring principles and structures, this chapter focuses on current strategy means to drive corporate evolution from traditional, longstanding systems to agileative, platform-based business models. The study investigates established enterprise architecture frameworks together with cloud-native architectural frameworks and hybrid architectural systems, and platform modernization techniques. The chapter investigates data integration methods together with interoperability requirements and microservices ecosystems that operate through API management systems. The elements establish the digital transformation architectural framework, which enables organizations to create platforms that can scale and withstand challenges while driving continuous innovation in the evolving digital environment.

2.2 ENTERPRISE ARCHITECTURE FRAMEWORKS

Organizations use Enterprise Architecture (EA) frameworks to create structured methods and reference frameworks that help them build their architectural systems. The growing complexity of digital transformation projects demands organizations to use structured methods for connecting their business goals with their information systems and data resources and technology systems. EA frameworks provide organizations with a structured framework which includes standardized domains and viewpoints and process definitions and governance systems to achieve architectural consistency throughout their various departments and projects. The frameworks present organizations with a comprehensive framework for understanding enterprise systems which enables them to track their strategic goals until they reach their day-to-day activities (Theseira, 2024).

Enterprise Architecture (EA) frameworks break down an organization into different architectural domains which include business architecture and data architecture and application architecture and technology architecture. The multiple layers of transformation projects ensure that different parts of the project connect with each other. Business capabilities drive application requirements; applications depend on data integrity and integration; technology platforms underpin performance, scalability, and resilience. The creation of EA frameworks establishes formal connections between different elements which helps organizations decrease duplicated work and reduce technical debt while they create their future development strategies. The usefulness of any framework depends on its successful implementation within an organization at various levels which include its business operations its sector of activity and its progress in digital technologies.

2.2.1 Conceptual Foundations of EA Frameworks

Enterprise architecture frameworks emerged as a solution to handle growing organizational complexity which developed during the late 20th century when organizations started investing more in IT systems. The initial attempts to create system architecture documentation developed into complete enterprise models which combined strategic elements with business processes and data movement and organizational systems. The discipline received its first major contribution from John Zachman who developed a systematic classification system that architects could use to arrange their design documents. His research established the basic ideas that other frameworks developed through his system of organizing things and his system of measuring all elements and his focus on different stakeholder needs.

Modern EA frameworks generally share several foundational principles:

1. **Holistic Enterprise View** – The architectural design needs to show the enterprise as a unified system instead of displaying it as separate independent projects.
2. **Multi-Stakeholder Perspectives** – Different stakeholders need customized perspectives which include executives' architects' developers and operations teams.
3. **Lifecycle Orientation** – The architectural design process develops through multiple iterations which continue until the final governance stage.
4. **Traceability and Governance** – Strategic objectives must be traceable to systems, services, and technologies.
5. **Standardization with Adaptability** – While structure is necessary, flexibility is essential to support agile and DevOps-driven environments.

These are some principles that are on which the major EA frameworks, used all over the world, are based.

2.2.2 Comprehensive Enterprise Architecture Frameworks

Comprehensive frameworks are designed to address enterprise-wide architecture across industries and organizational types. They typically provide structured methodologies, reference models, and governance processes.

A. **The Open Group Architecture Framework (TOGAF)**

   TOGAF stands as one of the most widely used enterprise architecture frameworks throughout the world because The Open Group developed and maintains it. The Architecture Development Method (ADM) serves as the main element that enables architects to progress through architectural development and governance processes using its step-by-step method. The architecture development methodology (ADM) consists of eight stages which include architecture vision, business architecture, information systems architecture, technology architecture, opportunities and solutions, migration planning, and implementation governance(Ardoq, 2024c).

   TOGAF requires organizations to establish their architectural repositories while managing their architectural documents through capability-based planning methods. The system operates effectively because it combines structured governance with its ability to function in different business environments. The system requires extensive customization to achieve operational efficiency because its extensive capabilities create difficulties that lead to excessive documentation requirements.

B. **The Zachman Framework**

   The Zachman Framework, introduced by John Zachman, is a taxonomy-based model rather than a step-by-step methodology. The framework organizes architectural artifacts through its two-dimensional matrix, which includes stakeholder perspectives and interrogative elements, which are used to display architectural artifacts. The system achieves its best performance through its ability to deliver complete results and its system of organized category definitions. The system requires organizations to use other methods because it lacks specific instructions for executing its implementation stages(Ardoq, 2024b).

2.2.3 Government and Industry-Specific Frameworks

Some EA frameworks were developed to address sector-specific needs, particularly in public-sector and defense environments.

A. **Federal Enterprise Architecture Framework (FEAF)**

The Federal Enterprise Architecture was designed to standardize IT investments across U.S. federal agencies. The system uses performance reference models and service component models together with technical standards to achieve operational interoperability and organizational accountability. The structured governance of FEAF system provides effective management for extensive regulated environments although it creates administrative challenges for private sector businesses.

B. **Department of Defense Architecture Framework (DoDAF)**

The US Department of Defense developed DoDAF to support mission-critical defense systems. The system delivers operational and systems and services and capability architecture assessments through its detailed viewpoint system. The system functions best in complex high-security environments because it requires traceability and reliability and long-term capability planning. The system becomes inflexible when used beyond defense applications.

2.2.4 Modeling Frameworks and Notations

ArchiMate

The standardized enterprise architecture modeling language ArchiMate exists to support The Open Group's TOGAF framework. The TOGAF framework establishes architectural development methods, while ArchiMate presents a standardized graphical system that shows business, application, and technology elements through their interconnected relationships. Architects use its layered modeling framework to demonstrate links between strategic goals and operational systems and infrastructure elements.

ArchiMate establishes common symbols and architectural viewpoints that help stakeholders understand architectural designs while decreasing uncertainties found in architectural documentation. The system provides multiple viewing options, which help executives, business analysts, and technical architects understand complex enterprise systems. The system requires architectural discipline and modeling expertise for effective implementation because detailed diagrams with poor organization become difficult to understand. ArchiMate implementation establishes better governance systems, which help businesses assess impacts while connecting their strategic goals with their technology execution.

2.2.5 Outcome-Driven and Advisory Approaches

Enterprise architecture frameworks make way for outcome-driven advisory methods which assess business metrics and examine strategic business connection. The methods which we use handle all project aspects through a combination of performance indicators and resource management and result evaluation. Organizations use architecture as a strategic asset which helps them achieve their goals through increased revenue and better operational efficiency and reduced risks and improved digital transformation results.

Digital enterprises that need to be agile and quick-moving will find these methods most useful. Organizations achieve ongoing technological alignment with their business goals through their architectural projects which result in measurable business value. The need for flexible systems to respond quickly to changing conditions requires organizations to establish governance frameworks which protect their systems from losing coherence and accumulating technical advantages. Advisory methods together with formal frameworks enable organizations to develop an architectural practice which achieves both structured operations and value generation.

Table 2.1: Comparative Analysis of Major Frameworks

Framework	Nature	Primary Strength	Limitation	Best Fit Context
TOGAF	Methodology-based	Structured governance & ADM	Can be documentation-heavy	Large enterprises
Zachman	Taxonomy-based	Completeness & clarity	No implementation process	Classification & analysis
FEAF	Government-focused	Interoperability & accountability	Administrative intensity	Public sector
DoDAF	Defense-focused	Capability traceability	High rigidity	Mission-critical systems
ArchiMate	Modeling language	Visual clarity	Requires a complementary framework	Architecture visualization
Gartner EA	Advisory model	Outcome-driven	Less prescriptive structure	Agile enterprises

Source: Developed by Author

2.2.6 Framework Relevance in Platform Modernization

The enterprise platform modernization process needs EA frameworks because they deliver the necessary structural discipline which enables organizations to move from their existing legacy systems toward building cloud-based modular systems. The TOGAF framework assists organizations with their migration planning needs while capability mapping requires TOGAF for implementation. Modern digital enterprises now use hybrid strategies that combine structured governance together with agile delivery methods to prevent the traditional architectural program rigidity which has existed in the past. Organizations need to develop their modernization strategy through adapting different frameworks because they should not depend on one specific framework. Organizations must achieve a balance between their official governance processes and operational flexibility because architectural standards should boost their digital innovation efforts. EA frameworks function as accessibility tools which enable organizations to implement scalable business changes through their usage of EA frameworks.

These frameworks lead organizations toward developing digital platforms that maintain compatibility with future technological advancements.

2.3 CLOUD-NATIVE AND HYBRID ARCHITECTURES

Cloud computing serves as the main element that supports enterprise platform modernization efforts. The architectural decisions organizations make for their cloud systems during digital transformation determine their ability to achieve agility and scalability and resilience and governance and long-term market competitiveness. Modern enterprise systems are primarily shaped by two architectural paradigms which include cloud-native and hybrid cloud architectures. The models function as deployment options which establish distinct methods for handling system development and system operation and system progress through innovative technologies (Susnjara, 2024).

Cloud-native architecture enables developers to create applications that function optimally in cloud environments through its use of distributed computing and automated processes and its modular design framework. Organizations use hybrid cloud architecture to combine their on-premises systems with both public and private cloud services which allows them to update their systems without losing their existing assets. The selection of these models depends on four factors which include regulatory restrictions and workload patterns and system development levels and organizational objectives. Enterprise architects and transformation leaders need to comprehend the basic distinctions between these two structures which have different strategic effects.

2.3.1 Cloud-Native Architecture: Concept and Design Philosophy

Cloud-native architecture describes systems which developers designed to function exclusively in cloud environments instead of systems which developers migrated from traditional infrastructure to cloud platforms. The architectural model uses microservices together with containerization and elastic infrastructure and automated deployment pipelines and API-based communication. Cloud-native systems use business capabilities as their base for building independent deployable services which break up application functions from their monolithic design.

The main characteristic that defines cloud-native systems is their ability to scale resources according to current user demands. The system automatically adjusts resource capacity to match user needs during peak times while it reduces resource expenses during periods of decreased system usage. The architectural design includes multiple security features which combine redundant systems with automatic recovery abilities and cloud-based service distribution. The system uses code-based orchestration frameworks to automate all infrastructure management tasks which include resource allocation and system setup and application deployment. Cloud-native systems operate with built-in flexibility which enables them to handle ongoing development work without interruptions.

2.3.2 Enabling Technologies in Cloud-Native Environments

The combination of advanced orchestration and virtualization with platform services creates cloud-native architectures. The process of containerization enables applications to be packaged with their required dependencies into portable units which can operate across different environments. The orchestration platform k8s implements automated containerized workload management through its capabilities for scaling and monitoring and failover handling. The orchestration layer provides a system to abstract infrastructure elements while allowing distributed systems to work together as a unified system.

The public cloud providers Microsoft Azure and Amazon Web Services deliver extensive platform services which enable users to implement serverless computing and managed databases and artificial intelligence integration and event-driven architectures. These services eliminate the requirement for infrastructure management which leads to faster application development processes. The cloud-native environment enables developers and architects to concentrate on business functionality because it delivers high abstraction levels together with operational activities.

2.3.3 Strategic Advantages of Cloud-Native Architecture

The strategic advantages which organizations gain from cloud-native architectural design transmit their effects beyond technical performance improvements. The adoption of cloud-native models enables organizations to achieve faster product delivery because they implement continuous integration and continuous delivery methods. Development teams can work on separate innovations because microservices use a modular design which decreases their need to share work with others. Digital business models which face unpredictable demand changes can rely on elastic scalability to support their operations which include e-commerce platforms and digital service providers. Organizations achieve cost savings through consumption-based pricing models which enable them to pay only for the resources they actually use. The cloud-native environments enable enterprises to distribute their services worldwide which allows them to enter new markets without needing to build extensive network systems. Startups and software-as-a-service providers and businesses which aim for rapid digital innovation use cloud-native architecture because of its specific benefits.

2.3.4 Hybrid Cloud Architecture: Structure and Operational Model

Hybrid cloud architecture functions as a unified computing system which combines on-premises infrastructure together with cloud-based resources. The hybrid architecture enables organizations to keep their important operations inside private data centers while using cloud platforms to achieve greater operational capacity and business analytical capabilities and development projects. The approach enables enterprises to achieve their modernization goals while maintaining their regulatory financial and operational obligations.

The hybrid model allows businesses to use their existing systems which include enterprise resource planning platforms and mainframe applications in controlled environments. The systems establish secure network connections with cloud services through the use of APIs and middleware. The hybrid architecture creates a system landscape which connects remote system components to enable organizations to implement modern technology one step at a time without needing complete system changes.

2.3.5 Enabling Platforms for Hybrid Architectures

The management system of hybrid cloud environments needs advanced management tools which can connect different infrastructure domains. VMware Cloud Foundation delivers unified infrastructure management through its integrated system of compute and storage and networking and security components which operate between private and public environments. Azure Arc provides organizations with a single platform to manage their operations while handling multiple systems throughout their business environment.

The tools enable enterprises to enforce their policies uniformly while maintaining their ability to move workloads between different systems and to monitor all activities from a single location which they need to operate their business across multiple system environments. The hybrid architecture needs strong governance systems together with sophisticated integration methods to stop operational fragmentation and complex system management.

2.3.6 Hybrid Architecture in Legacy Transformation

The primary reason organizations choose hybrid cloud solutions stems from their need to modernize outdated systems. Most large organizations maintain on-premises systems which they have developed over decades and which they cannot yet replace because of financial and legal and operational risk constraints. Organizations can use hybrid architecture as a bridge solution because it allows them to create API connections for their existing systems while moving analytics and reporting tasks into cloud storage and transforming their entire system design into separate functional elements. Organizations can pursue new cloud-based technologies while maintaining organizational stability because they can use this method as a step-by-step system modernization method. Organizations use hybrid environments to maintain better control over their confidential information which makes these systems appropriate for healthcare organizations and financial institutions and government entities that must follow strict compliance regulations. Therefore, organizations use hybrid architecture to create an operational link between their current IT systems and their complete transition to cloud-based operations.

2.3.7 Comparative Analysis: Cloud-Native and Hybrid Approaches

The fundamental distinction between cloud-native and hybrid architectures exists through their different infrastructure requirements and their varying complexity of operational procedures. Cloud-native systems achieve their goal of rapid development through automatic system expansion because they completely remove all physical infrastructure dependencies. The existing system requires complete system changes which need advanced DevOps skills to reach full operational capability. The management of hybrid architectures becomes more challenging because they require operation across two different environments. The framework of hybrid architecture enables organizations to execute their transformation at a slow pace while maintaining their ability to meet regulatory requirements and distribute their workloads across different locations.

The architectural choice between these approaches should not be viewed as binary. Organizations begin with hybrid models which they later increase to full cloud-native usage as their capabilities develop. The decision requires evaluation of four elements which include workload criticality, compliance requirements, investment constraints, and long-term digital strategy.

2.3.8 Governance, Security, and Cost Considerations

Automated identity management with infrastructure-as-code and zero-trust security models forms the core of cloud-native governance. The system implements security controls through deployment pipelines which maintain security across all distributed services. Hybrid governance requires organizations to synchronize cloud-native security systems with traditional perimeter-based security measures that protect their on-premises systems. The organization faces greater complexity in its operations because of dual governance systems but it gains more authority to manage its confidential operations. The two models establish different cost structures which result in different financial outcomes. The operational expenditure model used by cloud-native environments requires customers to pay based on their actual service usage while hybrid environments require organizations to spend both for on-premises equipment and for cloud-based operational expenses. The enterprise architects need to assess total cost of ownership during the complete application lifecycle instead of evaluating only the immediate infrastructure costs.

2.3.9 Architectural Decision Framework

The selection of proper cloud architecture needs an assessment method that follows established procedures. Organizations need to evaluate their regulatory requirements together with the levels of data protection needs and existing system dependencies and employee abilities and the difficulties of combining systems and their future business growth plans. A strategic architecture roadmap usually includes both cloud-native and hybrid components which help organizations decide where to run their workloads based on their business goals and acceptable levels of risk.

Hybrid architectural design functions as a temporary solution for various transformation initiatives while organizations work toward their ultimate digital-first capabilities through cloud-native architecture design. The governance of enterprise architecture establishes a systematic process for technological evolution which prevents organizations from adopting new technologies through uncoordinated methods.

Organizations can modernize their enterprise platforms through two different architectural approaches which include cloud-native systems and hybrid architectural designs. The distributed architectural system of cloud-native platforms enables organizations to attain rapid development and high scalability and swift innovation by utilizing automated and modular system design. Hybrid architectures enable organizations to modernize their systems in a controlled manner because they allow organizations to connect their existing systems with cloud solutions while meeting compliance requirements and transforming their operations. The future-oriented companies of today use both operational models together within their complete operational framework. The main goal of our work is to develop enterprise platforms which maintain continuous digital progress through their ability to work with other systems and withstand future challenges.

2.4 PLATFORM MODERNIZATION APPROACHES

Platform modernization describes the organized method which organizations use to update their essential technology systems so that they meet current digital requirements and their changing business needs. The process includes updating all components which build the enterprise applications and digital services including infrastructure systems and middleware technologies and runtime platforms and integration solutions and data management systems and operational support tools. The enterprise technology base undergoes platform modernization because it requires complete technology system transformation instead of making minor system improvements or implementing new technology. The system aims to achieve multiple goals which include reducing technical debt and enhancing system scalability through improvements to system resilience and system interoperability and establishing a cloud-based system which will enable ongoing innovation and support digital transformation efforts (Gaona, 2023).

Key Characteristics and Scope:

- The process requires changes that affect all architectural components, which include both backend infrastructure and middleware systems and integration solutions and data management tools and operational software.
- The process requires more than basic hardware upgrades or software updates because it needs fundamental changes in system design.
- The project will develop a technology base that contains modular components that provide service capabilities and work with cloud environments.

- The project functions as an extended strategic plan, which will remain active for extended times instead of being a quick technical solution.

Drivers of Platform Modernization:

- Customers now expect businesses to deliver digital experiences which provide instant access and continuous service and customized solutions.
- The business world requires companies to establish ecosystem connections which include their business partners and their suppliers and their external system vendors.
- The existing regulatory and compliance frameworks require organizations to implement more advanced security measures and improved governance systems.
- Businesses face competitive threats which force them to develop products faster while maintaining ongoing innovation for their existing products.
- The expenses for maintaining existing systems have risen because of outdated infrastructure and technology that no longer has vendor support.

Limitations of Legacy Platforms:

- Built on monolithic architectures with tightly coupled components.
- Designed primarily for stability and predictability rather than agility and scalability.
- Accumulate technical debt due to repeated patching and incremental updates.
- Difficult and costly to scale vertically through hardware expansion.
- Limited interoperability with modern cloud services and digital platforms.
- More vulnerability to cybersecurity threats by outdated security protocols.

Objectives of Platform Modernization:

- Reduce technical debt and operational inefficiencies.
- Enable horizontal scalability and elastic resource allocation.
- Improve system resilience through distributed and fault-tolerant design.
- Enhance interoperability through API-driven integration and standardized data exchange.
- Automated monitoring and patching together with compliance frameworks will help to enhance security.
- The system establishes a base which allows organizations to implement new technologies that include AI and analytics and cloud-native services.

Strategic Outcomes:

- Accelerated innovation and faster deployment of digital products and services.
- Improved operational efficiency through automation and orchestration.
- Greater alignment between IT capabilities and business strategy.
- Enhanced ability to participate in digital ecosystems.
- Establishment of a future-ready enterprise architecture capable of continuous evolution.

2.4.1 Drivers of Platform Modernization

The platform modernization process starts when organizations experience multiple strategic and operational and technological pressures. The primary driver of this demand exists because customers want better experiences. Digital consumers expect companies to provide them with smooth working systems that use their personal information to create customized experiences. Organizations face market demands because their legacy systems cannot handle multiple customer service channels and quick development of new product features.

Organizations need to modernize their systems because they want to create new revenue streams while enhancing their competitive strength. Organizations need to develop and launch digital products and services together with new business models at faster rates. Organizations experience product development holdups because their outdated systems prevent testing which leads to delays in product delivery which makes them more exposed to market competition threats. Through modernized platforms organizations achieve quicker product delivery times because they use automated systems which contain modular components and continuous delivery pipelines.

Organizations require system upgrades because their existing security measures do not meet current security needs. Organizations that use aging systems for their operations face a heightened risk of cyber threats because these systems contain unpatched security flaws and use outdated encryption methods. Organizations need to implement contemporary security frameworks which should use zero-trust security methods and automated threat detection and compliance monitoring systems to protect against rising global cyber threats. Platform modernization therefore becomes essential for safeguarding sensitive data and maintaining regulatory alignment.

Organizations need to handle two essential aspects of their operations because they require both scalability and performance. Organizations that use legacy monolithic systems face vertical scaling limitations because their systems require additional hardware to achieve growth which results in expensive and ineffective operations. Modern platforms use distributed systems architecture and cloud-based resources to allow horizontal scaling which maintains steady system performance during varying user demand times.

2.4.2 Architectural Dimensions of Platform Modernization

Platform modernization requires organizations to conduct architectural changes across all system components. The infrastructure layer of organizations enables users to select between virtual environments and cloud-based infrastructure and dedicated physical servers. The new system delivers three benefits which include flexible resource allocation and automatic system setup and efficient resource management. Modernization at the middleware and runtime system requires organizations to implement containerization and orchestration frameworks and managed platform services. The platform Kubernetes enables organizations to manage distributed workloads while maintaining consistent deployment processes throughout various operational settings. The public cloud systems of Microsoft Azure and Amazon Web Services deliver expandable infrastructure solutions and data services and artificial intelligence features which go beyond standard hosting methods.

Modernization at the integration layer replaces existing systems which use direct connections between endpoints with architectural frameworks that rely on APIs and event-driven messaging systems. The new design enhances system interoperability by decreasing system dependency issues while enabling users to connect with different platforms. Platform modernization for operational systems brings DevOps procedures and infrastructure-as-code solutions and automatic monitoring systems and ongoing security testing to operational systems. The organization uses operational systems to achieve continuous adaptability which goes beyond temporary changes.

2.4.3 The "R" Strategies Framework for Modernization

The "R" approaches, which describe different strategies, establish a common framework that people use to modernize platforms. The approaches establish a decision-making framework that organizations use to assess their existing heritage systems. The process of rehosting, which people call "lift-and-shift," enables organizations to transfer their applications from on-premises environments into cloud systems without making any substantial changes to their architectural design. The approach decreases infrastructure maintenance work requirements yet it still maintains existing monolithic system restrictions. Developers use refactoring to change their application code because they want to create better software that runs on cloud environments. The method becomes essential when organizations want to separate their monolithic applications into microservices or they need to handle their intricate legacy systems. Organizations gain more flexibility through their refactoring work even though this process needs more specialized technical knowledge.

Replat forming enables organizations to move their systems while selecting which components they want to optimize. Developers can modify applications to use managed database services and container environments and new middleware while the applications maintain their essential features. Organizations use repurchasing to replace their outdated systems with either commercial off-the-shelf software or software-as-a-service products. The approach becomes suitable for organizations that need to update their systems because their current systems no longer support their business requirements or because system upkeep costs have become too high. The process of retiring systems permanently eliminates outdated systems that no longer deliver operational advantages. The process of removing unnecessary elements helps organizations achieve two objectives, which include decreasing operational complexity and minimizing security risks. The process of retaining legacy systems enables organizations to keep certain systems operating because they find better value through cost advantages and required legal compliance. Organizations in these situations should direct their modernization initiatives toward enhancing integration capabilities instead of implementing complete system changes. The strategies that organizations use to achieve their goals do not compete with one another.

2.4.4 Platform Modernization versus Application Modernization

The process of platform modernization needs to be separated from the process of application modernization according to its definition. Platform modernization aims to update all core technological elements which include infrastructure, operating systems, and integration systems. The goal of application modernization is to redesign existing software systems through refactoring which leads to better user experience and system flexibility and enhanced operational capabilities.

The two projects work independently from each other yet they need each other to succeed. All modern application architecture functions at its optimal level when it operates on up-to-date infrastructure. Organizations will not achieve better agility results through infrastructure upgrades unless they also solve the problems caused by monolithic application architecture. Digital transformation succeeds only when organizations proceed to modernize both their platform and application systems.

2.4.5 Incremental versus Transformational Modernization

Organizations need to decide between executing modernization through step-by-step improvement methods or complete organizational transformation. The yardstick of incremental modernization helps organizations decrease their risk because organizations can make controlled system improvements that focus only on particular system parts. The operational process allows organizations to achieve gradual system migration through the implementation of the "strangler pattern," which replaces existing legacy systems with new operational services. Companies use transformational modernization to redesign their entire system architecture through cloud-native adoption and enterprise-wide replat forming projects. The digital capability development process allows organizations to implement new technologies at a faster rate but it creates additional operational costs and financial losses.

Organizations should select their correct strategy based on four factors which include their risk tolerance and available capital and their regulatory requirements and their need to maintain operational activities. The majority of enterprises implement a hybrid approach which combines immediate incremental modernization efforts with their ongoing commitment to long-term transformational initiatives.

2.4.6 Governance and Risk Management in Platform Modernization

The process of platform modernization creates governance problems that affect data integrity and service continuity and vendor dependency and compliance requirements. Modern enterprise architecture governance measures ensure that organizations achieve their business goals through their modernization programs, which require complete business operation alignment and current technology systems to function together. The process of risk management needs to address data migration accuracy, system integration reliability, security risks during transitional periods and the existing skill deficiencies within the organization. Organizations need to implement testing systems that include assessment frameworks and stakeholder alignment methods and workforce development programs to minimize operational disturbances during their modernization projects. Financial governance has equal importance to other financial management aspects. The total cost of ownership analysis must assess infrastructure expenses together with operational efficiencies and downtime reduction and innovation development and revenue growth possibilities.

2.4.7 Modernization and Digital Ecosystem Enablement

The present-day platforms deliver digital ecosystem access to users through their implementation of standardized APIs and their ability to scale data exchange and their support of cloud systems. The current business environment requires enterprises to operate through their connections with their suppliers and partners and their customers. The integration needs of ecosystem participation make it impossible for organizations to use their existing legacy systems.

The implementation of modular API-based system design enables organizations to share their internal services with external partners while they incorporate third-party products and utilize advanced data analysis tools. The transformation of the enterprise into a digitally connected organization occurs through ecosystem readiness, which establishes its presence in wider value networks.

2.4.8 Organizational Implications of Platform Modernization

The process of platform modernization requires technical upgrades which end up changing the entire operational structure and corporate culture of an organization. The implementation of DevOps practices enables development teams to work together with operations teams through their shared work duties. The process of automation decreases the need for humans to operate systems while it enhances responsibility through the use of precise performance indicators.

The workforce requires skill development for future job needs. The engineers need to acquire skills in cloud orchestration and containerization and security automation and distributed systems design. The leadership team needs to implement iterative planning methods together with continuous improvement systems to maintain their modernization efforts.

The process of digital transformation in enterprises relies on platform modernization because it acts as a fundamental component for enterprise development. The solution enables organizations to overcome their existing infrastructure problems together with their accumulated technical debt and their security weaknesses and their difficulties with system integration which stops them from achieving new technological advancements. Organizations can use the structured methods of rehosting and refactoring and replat forming and repurchasing and retiring and retaining to assess and enhance their outdated systems.

Organizations need to establish a complete architectural framework which includes governance controls and risk assessment processes together with their organizational capabilities for achieving successful modernization results. The process of platform modernization needs to become an ongoing development that builds enterprise strength and operational growth and market competitiveness in the digital business environment.

2.5 DATA INTEGRATION AND PLATFORM INTEROPERABILITY

Data and platform systems are vital to an organization as they are the critical elements that not only keep the business running but also allow it to develop new products and hence stay ahead of the competition. More and more organizations are committing their operations to distributed information systems and cloud services as well as mobile applications and IoT infrastructures and external partner ecosystems. At present, the organization is planning to invest in data integration systems that will allow different platforms to interoperate at their current level of operation.

The two capabilities of data integration and platform interoperability not only facilitate the sharing of digital systems but also allow them to fully understand the information that is exchanged among them throughout their entire operational system. Data integration methods standardize the data coming from a variety of sources while interoperability is the technical capability of two or more systems or components to communicate and share data and services through the use of a set of common standards and governance frameworks. The following section is a thorough academic review of the two concepts, their architectures, standards, maturity levels, benefits, tools and strategic implications (IBM, 2025a).

2.5.1 Data Integration

The process of data integration involves three sequential steps which create a unified data format that enables various analytical and operational tasks while supporting decision-making processes. Modern businesses create and store data across multiple platforms which include relational databases and cloud services and enterprise resource planning systems and customer relationship management software and spreadsheets and IoT devices and external application programming interfaces. The various data sources from different systems create data silos because they have distinct structural and semantic and data quality and storage attributes(IBM, 2025a).

Data integration serves to terminate data silos by achieving data consistency and providing unified access to data which supports reporting and analytical tasks and intelligent automation. Integration goes beyond simple data ingestion because it includes data cleansing and transformation and validation and governance and accessibility functions. The solution provides essential support for business intelligence and advanced analytics and artificial intelligence and digital transformation projects.

The Data Integration Process

The data integration life cycle usually comprises structured stage-wise endeavors to support data pertinence, validity and dependability:

- **Data source identification:** Organizations start their process by selecting all internal and external systems which provide them with necessary data. Their data sources include operational systems and software as a service platforms and historical databases and Internet of Things devices and system logs and external data streams.
- **Data extraction:** The system retrieves data through multiple methods which include connectors and APIs and database queries and flat-file transfers and streaming pipelines. The system can perform extraction in two different modes which are batch processing and continuous extraction for real-time operations.
- **Data profiling and mapping:** The profiling process assesses the quality of structure and data patterns which exist within datasets. The mapping process establishes connections between different system fields to maintain schema consistency throughout the system.
- **Data cleansing and validation:** Errors, inconsistencies and redundancies are identified and corrected. Standardization processes ensure uniform formats for dates, currencies, codes and identifiers.
- **Data transformation:** Data is converted into standardized schemas. Transformations may include normalization, aggregation, enrichment and format conversion to meet analytical or operational requirements.
- **Data loading:** Transformed data is loaded into centralized repositories such as data warehouses, data lakes or lake houses. Loading can be full-refresh, incremental or streaming-based.
- **Data synchronization:** Ongoing updates ensure that changes in source systems are reflected in target systems. The system commonly uses Change Data Capture (CDC) as one of its data tracking mechanisms.

- **Metadata management:** Metadata documents the origin, structure, transformation logic and meaning of data elements, enhancing transparency and traceability.
- **Governance and security enforcement:** Policies for access control, encryption, compliance and auditing are embedded within integration workflows.

Data Integration Architectures

Architectural patterns that organizations need to implement vary based on the scalability, performance and governance demands:

- **Extract, Transform, Load (ETL):** Data undergoes transformation processes before it gets stored in storage systems according to this method which requires comprehensive quality management and established operational control procedures.
- **Extract, Load, Transform (ELT):** The process starts with data being transferred to cloud platforms which can handle large volumes before data scientists transform it using the platform's computational abilities. ELT enables organizations to process both large data sets and high data volumes.
- **Real-time or streaming integration:** The system processes data immediately after its creation which allows users to monitor operational status through dashboards and detect fraudulent activities and control their Internet of Things devices.
- **Application Programming Interface (API) integration:** APIs establish a system that allows applications and microservices to share data in an ongoing manner.
- **Data virtualization:** A logical abstraction layer allows querying distributed data sources without physical movement.
- **Federated integration:** Queries are executed across multiple systems in real time without consolidating data into a central repository.

Each architecture presents trade-offs in latency, infrastructure cost, scalability and governance control.

Benefits of Data Integration

Effective data integration delivers multiple strategic advantages:

- Elimination of data silos
- Improved data quality and consistency
- Increased operational efficiency
- Accelerated access to insights
- Enhanced business intelligence and analytics
- Enablement of AI and machine learning initiatives
- Support for regulatory compliance and reporting

By establishing reliable and unified data foundations, organizations improve decision-making accuracy and operational resilience.

2.5.2 Platform Interoperability

The system requires less user involvement to establish data connections between various IT platforms and applications through its standards-based interoperability method. The system establishes both connection links between systems and shared understanding of the information that users exchange. Interoperability serves as a core requirement for organizations to work together across their internal departments and their external business partners and multi-industry networks. The system depends on standard technical specifications and data formats and communication standards and common vocabulary. In healthcare and public safety industries, these sectors require organizations to follow interoperability standards which ensure their systems will work together and continue to operate(Lindemulder, 2025).

Mechanisms of Interoperability

Interoperability operates through multiple coordinated mechanisms:

- Adoption of common data formats (e.g., XML, JSON)

- Use of standardized communication protocols
- Implementation of APIs as controlled interaction gateways
- Shared terminologies and taxonomies
- Metadata structures that define semantic meaning
- Governance agreements between participating organizations

Software developers implement these standards into platforms and provide documented APIs that allow secure and scalable system interactions.

Levels of Interoperability

Interoperability can be conceptualized across four progressive levels:

- **Foundational interoperability:** Enables basic data exchange without structured interpretation.
- **Structural interoperability:** Standardized formats allow systems to parse and process data fields automatically.
- **Semantic interoperability:** Shared vocabularies ensure that systems understand the meaning of exchanged data. The existing metadata structure at this level requires support from additional resources.
- **Organizational interoperability:** The system attains organizational interoperability when its governance policies and legal frameworks and operational procedures work together between different institutions.

The system demonstrates that interoperability goes beyond technical connections because it requires both semantic understanding and institutional partnership between organizations.

Strategic Importance of Interoperability

Interoperability offers organizations an array of benefits.

- Improved cross-system data accessibility
- Enhanced collaboration across departments and partners

- Reduced redundancy and operational inefficiencies
- Greater scalability of digital services
- Cost reduction through minimized system duplication
- Stronger ecosystem participation

The platform-based business models require interoperability as their essential requirement because it allows third-party developers and suppliers and partners to connect through standardized interfaces which enables ecosystem growth.

2.5.3 Integration of Data Integration and Platform Interoperability

The two concepts of data integration and interoperability remain distinct yet maintain a strong connection to each other. Data integration establishes clean standardized data through its process of transforming raw information into unified formats which organizations can use. Interoperability systems allow different platforms to exchange data while both systems maintain a shared understanding of that information. Data integration in enterprise architecture functions at both the data layer and application layer to consolidate all enterprise information resources for processing. Interoperability extends across three levels which include technical, semantic, and organizational boundaries to create standards and governance structures that support ongoing collaboration between different platforms.

Together, these capabilities enable:

- Real-time analytics across distributed systems
- Cross-organizational workflows
- API-driven digital ecosystems
- Cloud-native and hybrid platform environments
- AI-powered automation and intelligent services

The success of digital transformation projects in modern digital businesses depends on how well they combine their digital systems with their operational processes. Interoperability needs strong integration facilities because it depends on accurate data for successful operation. The implementation of integration processes requires systems to have open access points that connect to other systems. Current information systems architecture needs data integration and platform interoperability as essential building blocks. The process of data integration creates a unified data system for all users, while interoperability allows different systems and organizations to exchange information and maintain mutual comprehension. Enterprises that move towards cloud-native systems need to establish platform ecosystems that require AI-supported decision-making systems to function through their integration activities that must meet interoperability standards. The combination of two separate capabilities leads organizations to achieve better operational flexibility, which boosts their ability to grow and work together while developing new solutions for advanced digital environments.

2.6 MICROSERVICES AND API MANAGEMENT

The combination of microservices architecture and API management represents a major technological advancement which modernizes enterprise platforms. Digital enterprises require agility and scalability together with seamless ecosystem integration. This requirement has transformed architectural design from using monolithic systems to creating distributed service-oriented platforms which rely on standardized interface controls. Microservices enable businesses to break their operations into separate functional units while APIs serve as standardized communication interfaces to support system interoperability and governance and external system connections. The two elements create a new framework for enterprise systems which allows digital platforms to innovate continuously while maintaining operational resilience (Gallagher, 2025).

2.6.1 Evolution from Monolithic to Distributed Architectures

Enterprise application architectures have developed throughout history because businesses needed solutions for their growing complex processes and their ever-changing operational activities. The initial enterprise computing system used monolithic systems which required users to operate a single codebase that included presentation components and business logic and data layers. The architectures provided straightforward deployment options with total system oversight but their design structure prevented any alterations. The system required complete application stack duplication for scaling purposes while system updates required users to deploy the entire system anew. The system restrictions created operational problems which resulted in both reduced innovative development and increased operational risks.

Enterprises required more integrated systems when their operations expanded and digital channels started to multiply. Service-Oriented Architecture (SOA) emerged as a transitional model which introduced reusable services together with middleware-driven integration. The implementation of enterprise service buses created a centralized control system which established new operational bottlenecks that hindered business agility.

The architectural design of microservices provides superior distribution system development because it enhances existing distribution system design methods. It divides applications into separate deployable services that match business capabilities. The service components use lightweight communication protocols which include RESTful APIs and event-driven messaging systems. The transition from centralized monolithic systems to decentralized service structures leads to better system performance through expansion capabilities and shorter innovation timelines and better system error handling. The establishment of distributed architectures has completely transformed organizations together with their operational processes which now demand both technological and organizational changes.

2.6.2 Principles of Microservices Architecture

Microservices architecture operates based on basic principles which create distinct boundaries that separate it from traditional architectural methods.

- **Single Responsibility and Bounded Context**: Each microservice is designed around a specific business capability, adhering to domain-driven design principles. The services function within defined boundaries which help to establish system limits and decrease interdependencies between components.

- **Decentralized Data Management:** Microservices use a database-per-service model which differs from monolithic systems that typically share a single database. This design choice allows services to operate independently while maintaining separate data management systems.
- **Independent Deployment:** The system allows separate development and testing of services which enables their deployment without disrupting other system components. The system enables ongoing delivery while minimizing risks associated with product releases.
- **Lightweight Communication:** Microservices use lightweight protocols for their communication through HTTP/REST and messaging systems. The APIs establish formal rules for their communication methods.
- **Autonomous Teams:** Organizational alignment is critical. Cross-functional teams own services end-to-end, fostering accountability and accelerating innovation cycles.
- **Resilience by Design:** Microservices architecture includes built-in failure protection. The system should maintain full functionality when any single service experiences an outage.

The principles which guide this approach help organizations achieve operational agility while expanding their capacity to handle changing demands of digital business environments.

2.6.3 Core Architectural Components

A microservices ecosystem needs architectural components which provide three essential functions for system coordination and system expansion and operational system reliability. The distributed service deployment model requires infrastructure elements which enable communication handling and system monitoring and operational system recovery. The following components form the foundational support structure of a stable microservices platform.

- **API Gateway:** The API Gateway serves as the single point through which client requests access different backend services. The system handles multiple operational requirements which include user authentication and access control together with limitation of request frequency and combination of multiple requests. The system achieves better security protection and easier client handling and stronger governance mechanisms through its function centralization.
- **Service Discovery:** The discovery system for services operates as an ongoing process that updates its directory of active service instances together with their corresponding network locations. The system enables services to automatically find and connect with each other through dynamic endpoint discovery. The system enables containers to automatically adjust their resource needs while maintaining uninterrupted operations within their environment.
- **Load Balancers:** Load balancers distribute incoming requests across multiple service instances to optimize performance and resource utilization. The system achieves better availability because it redirects traffic from failed instances to operational servers. The system provides high reliability because it can effectively manage changes in workload demands.
- **Configuration Management:** Configuration management systems centralize application settings which enable services to access configuration data during their runtime. The system allows updates to occur without application redeployment which increases operational flexibility for users. The system maintains consistent operations between different environments while enabling organizations to meet their governance requirements.
- **Messaging and Event Brokers:** The dual purpose of messaging platforms exists because they enable asynchronous service

communication while they decrease system dependencies. The system enables event-driven workflows which allow services to publish and subscribe to events without needing direct connections to each other. The system improves distributed architecture performance through enhanced scalability and resilience capabilities.

- **Container Orchestration Platforms:** The container orchestration platforms handle automatic deployment and scaling process together with lifecycle management tasks of containerized services. The system achieves its high availability requirement through automatic instance restoration and resource management functions. The cloud-native environments depend on this automated process to sustain their operational stability.

The combined elements of these components establish the basic framework which enables distributed systems to operate reliably while maintaining their ability to grow.

2.6.4 Microservices Design Patterns

Microservices architectural design patterns deliver solutions to the typical challenges which arise in distributed system environments. The API Gateway pattern enables clients to access multiple services through a single interface which combines the results from different services. The Circuit Breaker pattern protects system stability by halting all system functions whenever certain services become inaccessible.

The Saga pattern establishes a framework that enables organizations to execute distributed transactions without establishing dependency on a central transaction management system. The system reaches its final state of consistency through its synchronized compensation processes that function across multiple services. The event sourcing system maintains permanent event logs to document all state changes which improve system traceability and auditing capabilities. "Command Query Responsibility Segregation" (CQRS) uses separate pathways for read and write operations which improve both system performance and system capacity. The patterns work together to create systems which can endure challenges while maintaining their operational efficiency through their complex nature.

- **DevOps, CI/CD, and Containerization**

  The system design of microservices architecture connects directly to DevOps operational methods and automated testing systems. The system enables automatic testing and service deployment through its continuous integration and continuous delivery pipelines. Microservices operate as self-sufficient units which match perfectly with incremental release methods because they help organizations to reduce deployment hazards while they boost their development speed. Containerization technologies package services together with their necessary runtime components which enables those services to function in different computing environments. Orchestration platforms handle all aspects of container management including their operational scheduling and system expansion and error recovery which leads to a decrease in needed workforce activities. The Infrastructure as Code system enables organizations to achieve reproducible results through its ability to create and manage their infrastructure resources through programming. The combination of microservices architecture and DevOps practices creates an environment which supports ongoing development work because it allows businesses to quickly adapt to changing market conditions.

- **Scalability and Resilience Engineering**

  Microservices architecture enables horizontal scalability which allows separate services to scale according to their operational needs. Organizations use cloud-native infrastructure to achieve flexible resource management which helps them minimize expenses while improving system efficiency. Microservices enable organizations to select specific services for scaling when their demand increases while monolithic systems force them to scale all application components. Resilience engineering addresses the vulnerabilities of distributed environments. The implementation of redundancy and timeout management and bulkhead isolation and graceful degradation techniques helps organizations reduce the effects of system failures. The observability frameworks enable organizations to monitor inter-service interactions through their logging and metrics systems and their distributed tracing capabilities. The architectural design of enterprises creates system resilience which enables them to maintain operational reliability and continuous service delivery during environmental changes.

- **Security in Distributed Systems**

  The distributed nature of microservices increases the attack surface, which requires organizations to implement complete security measures. API access security uses authentication and authorization mechanisms that security implement through OAuth protocols and JSON Web Tokens (JWT). Mutual Transport Layer Security (mTLS) enables secure service communication through encrypted data transmission.

  Zero-trust security models require verification for all interactions, which creates additional protection for systems because it does not trust any network location. Role-based access control restricts privileges based on defined policies, which helps organizations reduce the risk of insider threats. API gateways use rate limiting and traffic control measures to protect systems from denial-of-service attacks.

Development pipelines need DevSecOps implementation to integrate security which requires automated vulnerability scanning and compliance validation to be part of CI/CD workflows. The organization requires this security method because it ensures protection remains active throughout their systems instead of only responding to incidents.

2.6.5 API Management as Governance Infrastructure

The governance framework of API management enables organizations to control and standardize their distributed architecture system interactions. The uncontrolled use of APIs leads to inconsistent system behavior and duplicate resources and security risks as organizations expand their service offerings. API management platforms provide centralized functions for policy enforcement and authentication and monitoring and lifecycle management.

The essential functions of a system include gateway management and developer portal access and analytics dashboard display and version control system. Organizations use API contracts and usage policies to establish architectural guidelines that support their innovation efforts. API governance guarantees internal team and external partner interoperability which enables organizations to grow their operational ecosystem.

- **API Lifecycle and Ecosystem Control**

  The API life cycle establishes a fixed schedule which includes multiple phases starting from design work and proceeding through development testing deployment and monitoring until it reaches retirement. The standardized lifecycle management system maintains operational compatibility throughout its entire duration while minimizing service interruptions and ensuring real-time documentation updates. Versioning methods help to avoid sacrificing backward compatibility and, at the same time, allow continuous improvements. APIs enable organizations to share their internal functions through their systems which external users can access for engagement. Organizations use APIs to extend their operational capabilities through third-party developer access and business partner access and online marketplace integration. The platform-based approach enables an organization to transition from its existing business operation model into a complete digital ecosystem that drives both revenue growth and innovation development.

- **Risks: API Sprawl, Observability, and Complexity**

  Organizations experience fresh challenges through microservices and API-driven architectures despite their positive impacts. The expansion of services without centralized control leads to API sprawl which creates security vulnerabilities and operational difficulties. The debugging process and performance monitoring for distributed systems becomes more difficult because their service chains depend on each other.

Data consistency between services creates additional problems which become more difficult to solve when organizations need to maintain transactional integrity. The performance of services that communicate through synchronous methods will be affected by network latency. The combination of weak governance methods and inadequate monitoring tools will cause architectural fragmentation to diminish scalability advantages.

The implementation of architectural standards together with automated monitoring systems and established governance frameworks will establish a solution to these security pitfalls.

- **Strategic Role in Platform Modernization**

Modern enterprise platform strategies depend on both microservices systems and API management systems. Organizations achieve architectural agility and scalability through their practice of breaking down systems into independent modular components, which they connect through application programming interfaces. The system provides three key benefits, which include faster product testing, effortless partner connection, and adaptable business operations.

Microservices function as the fundamental framework that allows organizations to achieve modular transformation in enterprise platform modernization, while API management serves as the regulatory system that maintains system security and operational consistency. The two systems work together to transform traditional enterprise IT systems into flexible digital platforms that undergo constant development.

2.7 SUMMARY

The chapter examined architectural foundations together with modernization Techniques which enable organizations to convert their existing technology systems into flexible and expandable platform-based systems. The research started by examining various enterprise architecture frameworks which function as organizational blueprints for businesses to execute their strategic plans using technological systems. The research studied cloud-native and hybrid architectural models because they showed digital transformation capabilities through their flexible design and component-based system and distributed computing capabilities. The research investigated platform modernization strategies as architectural-driven processes which created adaptable technology systems while resolving existing technical debt. The chapter demonstrated how data integration and interoperability function as critical components which enable organizations to exchange information effectively between their sophisticated enterprise systems.

The chapter studied microservices together with API management because both components serve as fundamental elements that establish contemporary enterprise platforms. Microservices function as tools which enable organizations to develop independent modules that can expand their operational capabilities. The API management system functions as a security framework which manages system access while it protects data integrity and enables users to access all system components within the complete network. The two architectural methods create new enterprise systems which function as digital platforms that can undergo permanent transformation. The research demonstrates that organizations require both technological advancements and architectural management together with process automation to implement digital transformation strategies for their platform modernization efforts.

Multiple Choice Questions (MCQs)

1. **What is the primary purpose of Enterprise Architecture (EA)?**
   A. To design only IT infrastructure
   B. To align business strategy with IT systems
   C. To reduce employee workload
   D. To eliminate legacy systems
2. **Which of the following is a widely used Enterprise Architecture framework?**
   A. Scrum
   B. TOGAF
   C. Six Sigma
   D. DevOps
3. **What does TOGAF stand for?**
   A. The Open Group Architecture Framework
   B. Technical Organization Governance and Framework
   C. Total Operational Governance Architecture Framework
   D. Technology Oriented General Architecture Format
4. **Which characteristic best defines cloud-native architecture?**
   A. Monolithic design
   B. Tight coupling
   C. Scalability and resilience
   D. Single server deployment
5. **What is a hybrid architecture?**
   A. Only on-premises systems
   B. Only cloud-based systems
   C. Combination of on-premises and cloud environments
   D. Systems without integration

6. **Which approach involves breaking down a monolithic application into smaller services?**
   A. Virtualization
   B. Microservices architecture
   C. Waterfall model
   D. Batch processing

7. **What is a key benefit of platform modernization?**
   A. Increased system rigidity
   B. Improved scalability and flexibility
   C. Reduced system performance
   D. Elimination of APIs

8. **Which technology is commonly used for data integration across platforms?**
   A. APIs
   B. Firewalls
   C. Compilers
   D. Operating systems

9. **What is the primary role of API management?**
   A. Writing application code
   B. Managing and securing APIs
   C. Designing hardware systems
   D. Monitoring employee productivity

10. **Which of the following best describes interoperability?**
   A. Systems working independently
   B. Systems unable to communicate
   C. Systems exchanging and using information seamlessly
   D. Systems requiring manual data transfer

Answers

1	2	3	4	5	6	7	8	9	10
B	B	A	C	C	B	B	A	B	C

Chapter 3

Digital Technologies for Enterprise Transformation

3.1 OVERVIEW

Organizations achieve their digital transformation goals through advanced technology solutions, which expand their operational capabilities beyond standard automation systems and information processing capabilities. Modernization efforts require enterprise architecture to function as the fundamental structural design but organizations need to implement Digital technologies include sophisticated analytics, cloud computing, artificial intelligence, and the "Internet of Things" (IoT). and cybersecurity frameworks to achieve large-scale transformation. The technologies enable organizations to transform into data-driven operations that possess intelligent systems that can swiftly adjust to changing market conditions. Modern businesses attain their competitive edge through strategic management of their digital resources which function as interconnected systems across their entire operational framework (Stryker, 2025).

The chapter explores key digital technologies that are at the heart of business transformation and platform system upgrades. It begins with a discussion of Intelligent automation and artificial intelligence technologies that are the main drivers of improved decision-making and operational performance. Then the study identifies cloud computing and platform services as the backbone of business operations which give enterprises the freedom to digitally scale, and it goes on to IoT enablement which allows digital entities to interact with physical ones. The chapter looks into data analytics and decision support systems that facilitate the generation of insight, led enterprises, whereas cybersecurity and resilience strategies function as the organization's shield against the increasing number of digital threats. The integration of these technologies results in the key technological foundation that supports and empowers future, ready digital enterprises (SAP, 2025).

3.2 ARTIFICIAL INTELLIGENCE AND INTELLIGENT AUTOMATION

Enterprises use artificial intelligence (AI) and intelligent automation as their main technological foundations to drive digital transformation. Organizations can develop systems that learn and adapt through these capabilities instead of using traditional automated systems which only follow predefined rules. Businesses that operate online today use automation powered by artificial intelligence to achieve operational efficiency while using it as a key driver for their innovation efforts and ability to adapt and make decisions based on data. AI together with intelligent automation offers enterprises the required cognitive capacities and operational strength to thrive in ever-changing digital business environments because organizations today face more complex data challenges which include handling larger data sets at faster speeds. The section investigates how artificial intelligence and intelligent automation functions as the essential components which define enterprise platform modernization through its distinct conceptual foundations and technological elements and architectural designs and business advantages. The study investigates the governance and risk factors which must be considered alongside the ethical frameworks necessary for organizations to implement large-scale artificial intelligence systems.

3.2.1 Concept and Scope of Artificial Intelligence

Artificial Intelligence enables computer systems to execute tasks that normally need human intelligence functions, which consist of learning and reasoning and perception, verbal comprehension, and problem-solving skills. Artificial Intelligence systems improve their performance through experience because they process new data while traditional software systems maintain fixed operational rules. The operational value of AI systems derives from their capability to adjust their functions when facing unexpected circumstances which generate rapidly changing data.

Businesses use AI technology for their various operations which include customer analytics and fraud detection and predictive maintenance and supply chain optimization and personalized digital services. AI technology provides strategic advantages for organizations because it lets them convert raw data into valuable intelligence which they can use throughout their business operations. Organizations that successfully embed AI into their operational and decision-making processes are better positioned to achieve continuous innovation and competitive differentiation.

1. **Technological Foundations of AI:** The success of artificial intelligence in business setting is based on the combination of various fields of technology and collaborating with each other. The level of maturity of AI systems is dictated by the underlying technology on which they belong and defines how much the systems can scale to as well as how reliable they can remain in operation.

2. **Machine Learning (ML):** One essential component of AI systems is machine learning, which allow systems to recognize the patterns of the previously obtained data and generate forecasts or take decisions without involving direct coding. Some of the applications that companies use the ML algorithms include demand forecasting and risk scoring and recommendation engines and anomaly detection. Digital platforms use three different types of learning models which include supervised and unsupervised and reinforcement learning, to conduct various analytical tasks.

3. **Deep Learning (DL):** By using multi-layered neural networks that can process complex unstructured input, deep learning expands machine learning, types that include images and speech and natural language. Deep learning models enable

the development of advanced technologies which include computer vision and speech recognition and sophisticated pattern extraction. Organizations use deep learning technology during platform modernization projects because it helps them change manual cognitive workflows into automatic processes.

4. **Generative AI:** The field of generative AI research develops new models which generate original content that includes text and images and code and synthetic data. Enterprises deploy generative AI technology to automate content creation and develop knowledge assistants and speed up software development and improve customer interactions. Organizations face both productive possibilities and governance difficulties when they adopt enterprise platform systems.
5. **AI Agents and Autonomous Systems:** AI agents represent computer systems with the capacity to monitor their environment and make choices and perform tasks that help them complete their established objectives.

3.2.2 Intelligent Automation

Artificial intelligence and process automation are used to create intelligent automation technologies to create systems that not only perform tasks but also make decisions in a context, aware manner. The main focus of traditional automation systems was to perform tasks that were based on set rules through their repetitive operations. Intelligent automation allows automatic systems to update their knowledge and forecast future results, at the same time, they continue to perform their programmed tasks.

Companies have implemented intelligent automation as their operational requirements have necessitated them to keep their work processes running non, stop while at the same time they control costs and improve customer service through the use of increased employee capabilities. Firms are turning more and more to intelligent automation for the management of their highly complex processes that require them to deal with both structured and unstructured data across various stages.

The automation technology has been transformed, at first, it was concentrated on providing task, level effectiveness, and now, through intelligent systems, it is achieving a complete understanding of processes.

3.2.3 Core Components of Intelligent Automation

A mature intelligent automation ecosystem typically integrates multiple technological layers that work together to deliver cognitive and operational capabilities.

1. **Robotic Process Automation (RPA):** Repetitive, rule-based tasks are automated using RPA by mimicking human interactions with digital systems. The system functions through its use in data entry and report generation and transaction processing and system reconciliation tasks. RPA shows quick benefits but needs AI integration to achieve its maximum capabilities because AI allows bots to handle unpredictable situations.
2. **Artificial Intelligence and Cognitive Services:** The artificial intelligence components of computer vision, natural language processing, and predictive analytics help automation systems to process unstructured data and create context while supporting decision-making. These functions turn the deterministic workflows into the adaptive digital processes.
3. **Business Process Management (BPM):** BPM systems offer orchestration, workflow management and process visibility to complex enterprise processes. BPM, combined with AI and RPA, allows end-to-end intelligent automation of processes, making sure that automated actions will still be compliant to business rules and regulations. Process mining applications are used to analyze event logs to identify, track and optimize business processes. They assist the organizations in recognizing automation opportunities and gauge improvements in performance. Such a big data methodology helps to make sure that smart automation projects are based on operational reality and not assumptions.

4. **Enterprise Use Cases:** The implementation of AI and intelligent automation cuts across various sectors and business functions and yields quantifiable efficiency, accuracy and decision intelligence.

   - **Finance and Accounting:** Intelligent automation is applied in organizations to improve their financial activities that include invoice processing and account payable and account receivable reconciliation and cost validation. The AI-based fraud detection systems track transactions in real-time to detect any anomalous trends to reduce financial risk. The automated system complies with the regulatory reporting and financial forecasting of the system by the fact that the data is collected in different sources and the outcome will be superior compliance and correct forecasting of financial forecasts.

   - **Supply Chain Management:** The automation of supply chains based on AI environments enhances demand sensing because it allows to analyze the previous sales trends and market indicators and external factors. The dynamic nature of inventory optimization systems means that the level of inventory will be adjusted dynamically, thereby making it possible to keep its inventory level in optimal levels and get rid of overstocking and stockouts. The operational efficiency offered by the AI-powered logistics routing is the possibility to establish optimal transportation routes that help to minimize delivery time and minimize fuel consumption as well as distribution costs.

   - **Customer Service Operations:** The functions that are facing the customer are becoming more reliant on the use of AI-controlled chatbots and virtual assistants to provide customers with a personalized support system that is available 24 hours a day across multiple digital channels. The intelligent case management systems are automated systems that categorize service requests based on their priority levels and hence they can transfer requests to the respective teams thereby reducing the response times and increasing the success rates of resolutions. The capabilities that are developed enhance customer experience, reduce operational requirements that human support personnel have to address.

- **Human Resource Management:** Artificial intelligence-based talent assessment software is an application used by human resources departments to simplify the process of hiring new employees by automating resume scanning and candidate matching and first candidates research that is leading to quicker hiring durations. Workforce analytics platforms deliver predictive insights which help organizations assess employee performance and determine the likelihood of employee turnover and identify existing skill deficiencies, thus enabling organizations to develop effective talent management strategies. Employee experience platforms use artificial intelligence to deliver personalized learning suggestions and perform sentiment assessment and execute human resources service operations.

- **IT Operations and Infrastructure Management:** Intelligent automation in IT operations enables organizations to manage incidents before they occur through its ability to monitor systems and detect anomalies in all operational environments. Predictive infrastructure analytics help forecast system failures before they occur, reducing unplanned downtime. Advanced self-healing systems can automatically resolve typical problems through their ability to restart services and distribute system resources which results in improved system reliability and decreased need for human operation.

- **Cross-Domain Value Proposition:** AI and intelligent automation deliver their main benefits across all business operations through faster processing times and better accuracy and their ability to operate on a larger scale. The technologies allow organizations to make decisions based on data at a large scale while they minimize human mistakes in repetitive tasks and they enable their skilled workers to concentrate on more important strategic work. Organizations use intelligent automation as a basic system for digital transformation and competitive advantage which goes beyond its initial purpose of reducing operational expenses.

3.2.4 DevOps and Platform Integration Considerations

To provide long-term value, AI and intelligent automation should be closely associated with the current practices of DevOps and platform engineering. Model training, validation and monitoring stages are becoming more a part of Pipelines for continuous integration and deployment (CI/CD), emerging as the field of MLOps. The approach will ensure that AI models are accurate, explainable and comparable to evolving data conditions. Scalable deployment of AI services in the hybrid and multi-cloud environments are also improved with the use of containerization and cloud-native architecture. It uses API-led design and enables integrating AI into enterprise app, digital platforms and partner ecosystems. In the absence of such an architectural integration, AI projects will just remain isolated projects but not catalysts of enterprise-wide change.

3.2.5 Governance, Risk, and Ethical Considerations

Companies must implement a solution to the arising governance and ethical issues that will be brought about by the growing use of AI. The key problems that should be considered are the algorithmic bias and the model transparency and data privacy and regulatory compliance and the responsibility of decision made by automated systems. The dangers the poorly operative AI systems expose organization to outweigh the benefits the systems offer to the organizations.

Responsible AI frameworks set four main principles that comprise fairness and explainability and robustness and human oversight. Companies are establishing AI governance teams along with model risk management solutions and ethics review processes to realize credible AI implementation. A large number of jurisdictions are beginning to create new regulatory frameworks that require organizations to be more visible and have oversight of their automated decision-making systems. To achieve successful digital transformation, organizations require technological capability and rigid systems of AI governance.

3.2.6 Strategic Implications for Enterprise Transformation

Artificial intelligence and intelligent automation transform the existing working paradigm of contemporary business to the full extent. Organizations are embracing digital operations that are based on intelligent systems to develop processes that do not need human resources and operate based on certain events. The new business models along with hyper-personalized customer experiences and decision ecosystems in real-time makes companies run their businesses more efficiently. Strategic advantages that organizations reap in the AI-based technology hinge on the manner in which they execute it along with the enterprise architecture and data strategy and workforce transformation and platform modernization programs. Development of competitive advantage by automation projects is difficult since organizations must create improved automation systems. The industries that are leaders and pioneers in their respective fields take AI and intelligent automation as part of their platform functions that they incorporate across their entire system of technology.

The digital ecosystem growth will provide competitive positioning to businesses that develop industrialized AI frameworks and maintain good governance and architectural control since such organizations will gain operational strength and become digital peacekeepers.

3.3 Cloud Computing and Platform Services

The most significant technology architecture that has now become important in facilitating digital transformation processes in organizations is cloud computing. The technology allows the businesses to acquire the computing power by utilizing the internet that contains the servers, storage and databases, networking and analytics and applications in a pay-as-you-go model. The cloud solutions enable the companies to pay attention to value generation and operational flexibility because of the ability to cope with the complexity in the physical infrastructure. Cloud computing enables modern enterprises to handle their workloads because it provides them with flexible resources and expandable systems and efficient operational capabilities which match their increasing demands (Geeksforgeeks, 2025a).

Businesses use cloud platforms to improve application development processes while delivering services across different countries and using advanced analytics tools and creating testing environments through quick resource allocation. The combination of cloud computing using "Internet of Things" (IoT) technology, data analytics, and artificial intelligence has established itself as the fundamental infrastructure that supports modern digital platforms. The strategic value of cloud computing extends beyond its function as an infrastructure outsourcing solution because it creates a new paradigm for organizations to consume IT services.

3.3.1 Cloud Service Delivery Models

Cloud services function through three main service models which provide three distinct levels of operating systems and service delivery management requirements. The models need to be understood by businesses which create their cloud adoption plans and their efforts to update existing platforms.

Users can access virtual computational resources, including storage, virtual machines, and networking capabilities, through "Infrastructure as a Service" (IaaS) internet connectivity. The cloud provider maintains the physical infrastructure in this model while customers keep control over their operating systems and middleware and applications. Organizations which need to transfer their existing workloads and create particular runtime environments will find IaaS to be the most flexible option. The system enables organizations to employ lift-and-shift migration methods while they can dynamically adjust their computing power according to demand.

"Platform as a Service" (PaaS) offers businesses a comprehensive solution for creating and implementing the applications they want. Developers can focus on data and application logic without having to worry about infrastructure and runtime systems because the provider takes care of both components. The typical PaaS platform combines building software tools with middleware services and databases and automated resource management functions. This model enables development teams to work faster on creating software applications while spending less time on operational tasks which makes it suitable for developing cloud-native applications.

Users can access whole software programs through "Software as a Service" (SaaS), which they can access online through a subscription model. Users can access the software through web browsers or APIs while the system handles all backend infrastructure and platform operations. Enterprises use SaaS solutions to deliver their core applications such as human resource management, collaboration tools, "enterprise resource planning" (ERP), and "customer relationship management" (CRM) systems.

3.3.2 Hyperscale Cloud Platforms

There are a group of hyperscale providers that dominate the cloud computing landscape offering global infrastructure platform and enterprise and developer-specific capabilities. The Google, Microsoft Azure, and Amazon Web Services leaders are the most significant in the industry, App Engine. The platforms offer large ecosystems that allow organizations to implement all their processes of digital transformation

- **Amazon Web Services (AWS)**

  Amazon Web Services provides its customers with the most complete cloud platform, since it provides a full gamut of Platform as a service and infrastructure as a service offering. Businesses make advantage of AWS to access on-demand computing power together with storage and networking and database and analytics and machine learning capabilities. The global infrastructure of the system delivers high availability with geographic redundancy which makes the system ideal for handling critical enterprise operations.

Elastic Compute Cloud (EC2) functions as an essential AWS service that enables users to create and scale virtual computing environments. The platform provides multiple instance types which organizations can use to match their requirements for compute and memory and storage and GPU-dominated operations. The EC2 platform enables users to manage their workloads through quick resource allocation and automated resource scaling and deployment via image templates.

The Simple Storage Service S3 functions as AWSs primary object storage solution which provides exceptional durability. The system enables enterprises to store and retrieve data through APIs and management consoles without any restrictions on data volume. Organizations commonly use S3 to create data lakes and to store backups and archival content and to distribute content and to build analytics pipelines. AWS provides a complete cloud solution through its managed databases and caching services and identity management system and DNS and load balancing and content delivery services which go beyond EC2 and S3.

AWS delivers multiple key benefits to customers through its highly elastic system and its extensive network of global availability zones and its extensive service offerings and its pricing system which charges customers based on their actual resource consumption.

- **Google App Engine (GAE)**

  Developers can construct and launch web apps with Google App Engine's Platform-as-a-Service offering that can scale their operations. The system creates an automatic scaling mechanism which controls system resources by matching usage requirements of the application. The solution works best for businesses which need to develop products quickly while spending as little time on maintenance as possible.

The platform delivers a secure runtime environment which includes essential features such as in-memory caching and scalable data storage and messaging systems and job queue management and scheduled task handling. Developers can build and test applications locally using the App Engine SDK which emulates the production cloud environment. The system allows developers to choose from multiple programming languages which include Python Java and Go for software development.

Google App Engine provides its main advantages through automatic scaling functions which simplify deployment processes and its strong connection to the entire Google Cloud platform. The system works best for services which operate as cloud-based web applications and mobile application backend systems.

- **Microsoft Azure**

  Microsoft Azure offers businesses a complete cloud computing platform that includes "Infrastructure as a Service" (IaaS) and "Platform as a Service" (PaaS) functions. Organizations can create, launch, and control their applications through Microsoft Azure which operates from its worldwide network of data centers. Azure attracts enterprises that already use Microsoft technologies because it provides seamless connections to Visual Studio, .NET, and Active Directory software tools.

  Distributed systems use role-based structures to design Azure applications which operate as their main system components. The platform provides multiple services which include cloud storage, networking, content delivery networks, caching systems, identity and access management solutions, plus advanced security features. Organizations use Azure hybrid cloud support to combine their on-premises systems with digital cloud resources which makes it the top choice for businesses in regulated sectors that want to switch to cloud solutions progressively.

Azure brings businesses three main benefits which include advanced security for enterprises, the ability to deploy systems through multiple methods, and complete compatibility with Microsoft software solutions.

3.3.3 Big Data Platforms in the Cloud Ecosystem

The cloud-based data processing architectures to which Apache Hadoop is a fundamental element are not independent cloud platforms by themselves. An open-source distributed computing framework, Hadoop allows users to run data processing operations on massive-scale datasets over multiple standard hardware clusters. It employs the MapReduce programming model which permits data processing in parallel, thus ensuring the application of a fault-tolerant system.

Hadoop Distributed File System (HDFS) offers highly available storage capability by spreading copies of the data over various nodes, which not only guarantees availability of the data but also protects the data from loss by hardware failure. The MapReduce framework facilitates very large-scale parallel processing through its two-stage computation process, which comprises the map and reduce steps. The flexible resource scaling and on-demand storage services provided by a cloud infrastructure make it very suitable to Hadoop scenarios that are companies' choice for their core operation. Hadoop facilitates the handling of massive datasets very efficiently while its open-source nature provides organizations with affordability. The implementation of the system in conjunction with cloud platforms has made it a key player in big data ecosystems.

3.3.4 Enterprise SaaS and Platform Ecosystems

Enterprise SaaS platforms deliver business functionality through completely managed environments because cloud computing technology enables their development. Salesforce uses its Force.com platform to provide developers with a PaaS environment for enterprise application development while offering CRM solutions through SaaS.

Force.com enables developers to build business applications by using its existing workflows and data models and user interface components. The platform provides complete system functionality through web services APIs which permit users to connect with both cloud and on-premises systems. The cloud environment enables organizations to achieve automatic resource scaling and continuous system operation while decreasing their need to manage physical infrastructure.

The Salesforce ecosystem provides businesses with three main benefits which include fast application development through code-free methods and strong system connections and access to established enterprise SaaS products. Cloud computing enables businesses to deliver complete operational functions through its platforms which extend beyond basic infrastructure services.

3.3.5 Strategic Importance in Enterprise Transformation

Cloud computing and platform services constitute essential components for modernizing business operations. Organizations can use these platforms to shift from traditional infrastructure spending to flexible usage-based financial systems which enhance their ability to manage expenses and their operational resources. The key role of cloud platform is to provide the necessary technological infrastructure through which organizations can create new capabilities that involve artificial intelligence and advanced analytics and IoT integration and digital ecosystem involvement.

The cloud architectural structure allows organizations to use microservices and automate the DevOps operations and construct continuous delivery pipelines and generate API-driven structures. The organization achieves improved flexibility through these capabilities which expedite the development of new products. Cloud platforms enable businesses to extend their digital services worldwide because they allow companies to enter new markets without needing major infrastructure expenditures.

Organizations must establish proper governance systems to succeed with cloud adoption which should include performing workload evaluations and managing expenses and developing security systems and ensuring compliance and selecting vendors. Companies create hybrid and multi-cloud systems to achieve operational flexibility while maintaining business continuity and reducing their exposure to vendor-related dangers.

Cloud computing with platform services has become essential for businesses to achieve their digital transformation goals. Organizations use cloud platforms to create new products through their elastic infrastructure and managed development environments and complete business applications which enable them to operate efficiently. Modern digital enterprises depend on hyperscale providers together with big data frameworks and enterprise SaaS platforms which create their essential technological infrastructure.

Cloud computing will remain important for organizations to choose platform architecture solutions as they upgrade their older systems and implement data-based strategies. The technology will reshape enterprise digital service creation and implementation processes through its upcoming combination with artificial intelligence and automation and distributed computing systems.

3.4 INTERNET OF THINGS (IOT) ENABLEMENT

The IoT enablement is an essential feature of the modern digital businesses, and it allows organizations to integrate physical assets, spaces, and devices into a data-driven smart ecosystem. The IoT turns the operations, which used to be isolated, into the processes that are constantly observed and optimized by connecting sensors, software, and network access to commonplace items and industrial equipment. This section explores how IoT enablement supports real-time visibility, automation, predictive decision-making, and new digital business models. As enterprises accelerate their digital transformation journeys, effective IoT enablement becomes critical for unlocking operational efficiency, enhancing customer experiences, and creating scalable, data-centric innovation across industries (IBM, 2025b).

The "Internet of Things" (IoT) is a network of physical objects, such as automobiles, appliances, and other goods, that are outfitted with sensors, software, and network connectivity to collect and share data. Internet ofThings devices, sometimes known as"smart objects,"can range from wearables like smartwatches and clothing with RFID capabilities to complex industrial machinery and transportation systems. Technologists are even envisioning entire "smart cities" based on IoT technologies.

IoT enables allow smart devices to interact with other internet-enabled devices as well as with one another. similar to smartphones and gateways, establishing an extensive network of linked devices with the ability to share information and carry out different tasks on their own. This may consist of:

- Monitoring the environmental conditions in agriculture
- Managing traffic patterns with smart automobiles and other smart vehicle technology
- Overseeing plant machinery and processes
- Keeping an eye on warehouse inventory and shipments

IoT has many potential applications, and several industries, including manufacturing, transportation, healthcare, and agriculture, are already experiencing its effects. As the number of internet-connected devices continues to increase, IoT is predicted to have a greater influence on the way our world is shaped. altering the way we live, work, and interact with each other. IoT devices in a corporate environment monitor a wide range of data, such as temperature, humidity, air quality, energy consumption, and machine performance. Businesses can boost productivity and profitability by identifying trends, patterns, and anomalies in this data through real-time analysis.

What makes IoT significant?

IoT matters to businesses for several reasons. The primary benefits of IoT are as follows:

1. **Improved efficiency:** By using IoT devices to automate and optimize processes, businesses may boost efficiency and productivity. For example, IoT sensors can be used to monitor equipment performance and detect or even address potential

issues before they cause downtime, reducing maintenance costs and increasing uptime.

2. **Data-driven decision-making:** IoT devices provide vast amounts of data, which may be used to create new business models and improve decision-making. By analyzing this data to get insights into consumer behaviour, market trends, and operational performance, businesses may make better decisions about strategy, product development, and resource allocation.
3. **Cost-savings:** By automating repetitive tasks and reducing human processes, IoT can help businesses save costs and boost profitability. For example, IoT devices can be used to monitor and optimize energy use, reducing energy expenditures and promoting sustainability.
4. **Enhanced customer experience:** By using IoT technology to gather information about customer activity, businesses can provide their customers more personalized and engaging experiences. For example, merchants can employ IoT devices to track customer movement within their stores and make offers that are specific to their behaviour.

3.4.1 The technologies that enable the Internet of Things

IoT is made feasible by a number of technologies working together.

- **Sensors and actuators:** Devices known as sensors are able to detect changes in the following environmental parameters: motion, temperature, light, humidity, and pressure. Actuators are devices that can physically change their environment, such as starting a motor or opening or closing a valve. These devices are crucial to the Internet of Things because they enable communication between machines and devices and the physical world. Automation is made feasible when sensors and actuators work together to solve issues without requiring human intervention.

- **Connectivity technologies:** For sensors and actuators to transmit data to the cloud, IoT devices need to be online. Numerous networking technologies, including LoRaWAN, Zigbee, Bluetooth, cellular, and wifi, are used by the Internet of Things.
- **Cloud computing:** The cloud handles the processing, storing, and analysis of the massive amounts of data generated by IoT devices. Cloud computing platforms offer the infrastructure and tools needed to store and analyze this data as well as to create and deploy IoT applications.
- **Big data analytics:** To find patterns and extract insights from the vast amounts of data generated by IoT devices, businesses need to use advanced analytics technologies. These resources could include machine learning algorithms, data visualization tools, and predictive analytics models.
- **Security and privacy technologies:** As IoT installations proliferate, IoT security and privacy become increasingly important. Technologies like encryption, access controls, and intrusion detection systems protect IoT devices and the data they generate from cyberthreats.

Examples of IoT applications

A. **Healthcare:** In the healthcare industry, IoT devices can be used to remotely monitor patients and collect real-time data on their vital signs, such as heart rate, blood pressure, and oxygen saturation. By analyzing this sensor data, patterns may be found and any health issues can be identified before they get worse. IoT devices can also be used to monitor medication compliance, track medical equipment, and manage inventory.

B. **Manufacturing:** Industrial IoT devices can be used in manufacturing to monitor machine performance, spot equipment issues, and expedite production processes. For example, sensors can monitor temperature and humidity at a manufacturing facility to ensure that the proper conditions are fulfilled for the production of sensitive goods. IoT devices can also be used to monitor the quality of finished goods, manage supply chains, and maintain inventory.

C. **Retail:** In the retail industry, IoT devices can be used to monitor inventory levels, track customer activity, and optimize store layouts. Using sensors to track foot traffic in a store and assess customer activity, for example, retailers can improve the customer experience and optimize product placement. Additionally, IoT devices can be used to monitor supply chains, track shipments, and manage inventory levels.

D. **Agriculture:** IoT devices can be used in agriculture to monitor soil conditions, weather trends, and crop development. For example, sensors can be used to measure the moisture content of the soil, ensuring that crops are irrigated at the right moment. IoT devices can also be used to monitor animal health, manage supply chains, and track equipment. Low-power or solar-powered gadgets can often be used in rural settings with minimal monitoring.

E. **Transportation:** In the transportation sector, IoT devices can be used to track goods, improve routes, and keep an eye on vehicle performance. For instance, sensors can be used to track connected cars' fuel efficiency, which lowers fuel expenses and increases sustainability. In order to guarantee that cargo reaches its destination in optimal condition, IoT devices can also be utilized to monitor its condition.

3.4.2 Risks and challenges in IoT

In addition to its many benefits, IoT has a number of hazards and challenges. Some of the most significant ones are as follows:

1. **Security and privacy risks:** As the number of IoT devices increases, security and privacy are becoming increasingly important. Sensitive data on many IoT devices can be compromised by hackers and other cyberthreats. IoT devices have the potential to collect vast amounts of personal data, which presents privacy and data security challenges.

2. **Interoperability issues:** IoT devices made by different manufacturers usually use different standards and protocols, which makes it difficult for them to talk to one other. This could lead to interoperability issues and difficult-to-integrate and evaluate data silos.
3. **Data overload:** Companies that are ill-prepared to handle the enormous amounts of data produced by IoT devices risk being overloaded. Analyzing this data and drawing practical conclusions can be challenging, especially for businesses lacking the necessary analytics expertise and resources.
4. **Cost and complexity:** Implementing IoT systems may be costly and challenging, requiring significant investments in hardware, software, and infrastructure. IoT system maintenance and administration can be challenging and require specialized skills and knowledge.
5. **Regulatory and legal challenges:** There are growing legal and regulatory issues as IoT devices proliferate. Companies must abide by a number of cybersecurity, privacy, and data protection laws that differ from nation to nation.

How should businesses approach IoT?

Controlling IoT devices may be a complicated and difficult process, yet, a few best practices may be implemented by a business to guarantee that its IoT devices are dependable, safe, and focused on performance. Some advice for handling IoT devices is as follows:

1. **Plan your IoT strategy:** Before deploying any IoT devices, businesses should have a solid understanding of their objectives, use cases, and desired outcomes. By doing this, businesses can choose the right IoT platforms, devices, and technologies and ensure that their IoT strategy aligns with their business goals.
2. **Choose secure IoT products:** The IoT solutions also presuppose security as it can be exposed to cyberattacks. The current businesses are supposed to select the device that is security-

oriented and apply the proper security measures including access controls, authentication, and encryption.

3. **Monitor and maintain devices:** To make sure they are operating at their best and are not susceptible to security risks, IoT devices require routine maintenance and monitoring. This may entail doing routine security audits, predictive maintenance, firmware and software updates, and device health and performance monitoring.
4. **Manage data effectively:** IoT devices generate massive amounts of real-world data, which can be challenging to manage and assess. Businesses should have a clear data management strategy that addresses data storage, analysis, and visualization. to ensure that the data generated by their Internet of Things devices may yield meaningful insights.
5. **Build an ecosystem:** IoT devices are often part of a larger ecosystem that includes different devices, platforms, and technologies. Businesses should be knowledgeable about this ecosystem and ensure that their IoT devices are compatible with other systems and technologies.

The future of IoT

IoT has a bright future ahead of it, with plenty of innovative business-related advancements to come. These are some of the IoT's future trends and projections:

- **Growth:** Tens of billion It is anticipated that the number of IoT devices will continue to rise rapidly over the coming years. This growth will be fueled by increased industry adoption as well as the development of new use cases and applications.
- **Edge computing:** Edge computing is becoming increasingly important for the Internet of Things because it makes it possible to handle and analyze data closer to the data source rather than in a centralized data center. This can reduce latency, accelerate response times, and reduce the amount of data that needs to be transmitted via IoT networks.

- **Artificial intelligence and machine learning:** AI and machine learning are becoming increasingly important in the context of the Internet of Things because they can be used to analyze and extract useful insights from the vast amounts of data generated by IoT devices. This can help businesses make better decisions and streamline processes.
- **Blockchain:** Researchers are looking into using blockchain technology to improve the security and privacy of the Internet of Things. Blockchain technology can be used to create secure, decentralized networks for Internet of Things devices, thereby reducing data security vulnerabilities.
- **Sustainability:** Sustainability is gaining importance in IoT as businesses look for ways to reduce their environmental impact. IoT can be used to increase sustainability, reduce waste, and maximize energy use in a range of businesses.

3.5 DATA ANALYTICS AND DECISION SUPPORT SYSTEMS

Organizations now choose strategic paths through their accumulated evidence instead of relying on their previous judgment methods. Organizations today face operational challenges because they must handle three main factors: excessive data, unpredictable market changes, and fast-moving digital transformation. Organizations now consider Data Analytics and Decision Support Systems (DSS) as essential capacities which help them achieve their operational improvement goals and their ability to respond to changing business needs. The technologies here work together to help businesses transform their unprocessed data into usable insights that enable their executives to make quick decisions based on reliable information which they can defend (Shad, 2023).

Data analytics functions as the main operational framework which uses scientific methods to transform both organized and disorganized data into meaningful insights. Data analytics functions as the main operational framework which uses scientific methods to transform both organized and disorganized data into meaningful insights. Decision Support Systems deliver structured methods which enable users to access knowledge that helps them make choices. The combination of analytics and DSS systems creates a closed-loop decision-making system which uses data to guide every step from planning to execution and monitoring and optimization. This section provides a detailed analysis of modern enterprises that combine data analytics with decision support systems through their architectural structure their functional techniques and their strategic business advantages.

3.5.1 Foundations of Data-Driven Decision Support

Decision support systems were initially designed to assist managers in making semi-structured decisions by providing data and models through user-friendly interfaces. The original DSS platforms dedicated their resources to creating basic modeling tools which enabled users to generate reports. The combination of big data and machine learning advancements together with real-time data stream expansion has built up new DSS capabilities which now include better advanced features. The data analytics adoption in modern business settings transform DSS into a system that functions based on historical data analysis into an instrument with predictive and prescriptive decision-making abilities. DSS platforms that are analytics-friendly facilitate organizations to do more than summarizing events and give organizations insights into the causes of events and their future progression and how to get their optimal outputs.

These capabilities combination promotes a number of strategic goals. The data analytics adoption in modern business settings transform DSS into a system that functions based on historical data analysis into an instrument with predictive and prescriptive decision-making abilities. DSS platforms that are analytics-friendly facilitate organizations to do more than summarizing events and give organizations insights into the causes of events and their future progression and how to get their optimal outputs.

This importance is part of the larger story of the rise of some strategic goals.

- Improving decision accuracy and consistency
- Reducing time-to-decision

- Enhancing organizational responsiveness
- Enabling proactive risk management
- Supporting data-driven culture transformation

As digital enterprises are built and expanded, the case for entrenching analytics within decision processes could not be clearer.

3.5.2 Role of Data Analytics in Enhancing DSS

Data analytics extends its support to Decision Support Systems throughout the entire information lifecycle which includes both data acquisition and insight delivery processes. The three main layers of the system show how it affects work operations.

- **Data acquisition and preparation:** The analytics pipelines deliver high-quality and relevant data to DSS platforms because they maintain their data quality. The existing systems use automated processes for data cleansing and normalization and enrichment, which improve the accuracy of their subsequent decision-making processes. The project aims to develop information assets which can be used to make decisions instead of collecting new data.
- **Analytical processing:** The analytical engine functions as the central component of advanced DSS systems. The process begins with raw data which transforms into useful patterns and prediction results through the application of statistical models and machine learning algorithms and optimization techniques. The DSS system achieves its strategic worth through the development of advanced analytics capabilities which enable organizations to conduct deep analytical work.
- **Insight delivery and visualization:** The method which presents insights to users holds critical valueThe data analytics process creates value for decision support systems through its development of interactive dashboards and visual storytelling tools and its ability to detect anomalies and simulate different scenarios. Effective visualization design enables users to

process information with less cognitive effort while decision-makers at all organization levels can quickly comprehend the presented data. The improved capabilities of DSS transform it into an intelligent decision support system which functions beyond its basic reporting capabilities.

3.5.3 Core Components of an Effective DSS

A Decision Support System reaches its maximum strength through the combination of multiple essential components which work together as a single unit. The system gains greater strength through the addition of modern analytics functions to its individual components.

- **Data management layer:** This would be a hypothetical system given the consensus of their assistance in decision-making. Good-performing DSS environments focus on data quality, lineage tracking, metadata management and governance controls in order to build trust on decision outputs.
- **Model management layer:** Analytical models, simulation engines, forecasting tools and optimization algorithms are found in the model layer. More and more this layer will include machine learning pipelines that retrain themselves based on new data, allowing an adaptive decision support.
- **Knowledge management layer:** DSS systems require numerical analysis together with business logic and business knowledge and business heuristics for their advanced functionality. The contextual intelligence system guarantees that all recommendations create a proper alignment with both organizational policies and regulatory restrictions.
- **User interface and visualization layer:** Adoption depends on the front-end experience. Current DSS interfaces also provide role-based dashboards and natural language querying and mobile viewing capabilities. The concept of self-service analytics has gained special significance in the democratization of the decision support at the enterprise level.

- **Integration and workflow orchestration:** Enterprise DSS systems do not function as independent systems. Their operation requires integration with ERP systems and CRM systems and supply chain systems and operational systems. Automated responses or approvals or notifications can be generated through workflow orchestration, which connects the analysis process with the implementation of executive decisions.

The combination of these elements creates a unified ecosystem that underpins elaborate decision settings.

3.5.4 Analytics Techniques Powering Decision Support

The very foundation of the success of decision support systems through analytical approaches lays in the analyses. There are three types of analytics that have complementary but separate role.

- **Descriptive analytics:** The descriptive methods provide an overview of historical performance and situational awareness. Dashboards, scorecards, and trend analyses can assist organisations with the knowledge of what has occurred and define performance baselines. Descriptive analytics alone is not enough to have competitive advantage, but it is a foundation.
- **Predictive analytics:** Predictive models apply the historical trends to make the future predictions. Regression modeling, time-series forecasting, and machine learning classification are some of the strategies that organizations are able to predict demand variations, customer churning, equipment breakdown, and financial risks. Predictive ability is a great help in the accuracy of planning.
- **Prescriptive analytics:** The highest level of decision intelligence is prescriptive analytics. The prescriptive systems prescribe a given course of action by overlaying the predictive outputs with optimization algorithms and business constraints. The system provides three functions which include dynamic pricing suggestions and inventory optimization and resource

allocation strategies. DSS advisory tools will transform into decision automation tools because of this capability. Organizations that successfully implement the three layers achieve their highest strategic benefits.

3.5.5 Real-Time and Streaming Decision Support

Real-time intelligence is one of the biggest developments concerning DSS. Decisions of sixth-ranking in digital commerce, financial trading, cybersecurity, industrial operations, etc., must be made in seconds or even milliseconds.

Real-time analytics allow DSS platforms to accept real-time data streams of operational systems, IoT devices, customers, and external feeds. The use cases that can be supported with this capability include:

- Fraud detection during financial transactions
- Predictive maintenance in smart factories
- Dynamic pricing in e-commerce
- Real-time supply chain visibility
- Network and security threat monitoring

The move toward real-time decision support requires robust event-streaming architectures, in-memory processing, and edge analytics capabilities. The organizations should also solve the problem of latency, data consistency, and scalability issues to enjoy the benefits fully.

3.5.6 Enterprise Applications and Business Value

In industries, DSS platforms that are enabled by analytics are producing quantifiable business value.

Risk modeling, credit scoring and monitoring of regulatory compliance is an example of an area where advanced DSS are used by organizations in finance. Decision support tools help in optimization of inventory levels, logistics routing, and demand planning in supply chain management. Customer analytics and recommendation engines are used by the marketing team to segment and tailor the interaction with the customer and enhance the conversion rate. Workforce analytics are applied in the human resources departments in talent acquisition, retention, and productivity planning. Intelligent DSS platform is used in IT operations to help predict incidents, do capacity planning, and automatically remediate.

The typical value drivers are: enhanced operational efficiency, less uncertainty, more rapid response times and increased strategic focus. Perhaps more crucially, the use of DSS will help in the overall cultural change to data-oriented management.

3.5.7 Challenges in Implementing Analytics-Driven DSS

Although analytics-enabled Decision Support Systems have potential to transform organizations, there are various organizational and technical issues that come with implementation of analytics-enabled systems.

- **Data complexity and quality issues:** Enterprises tend to experience disintegrated, irregular, or low-quality data. In the absence of good data governance, the output of DSS can be a false alarm.
- **Integration barriers:** DSS integration can be facilitated by legacy systems, siloed architectures and non-compatible data formats that can make integration across the enterprise technology landscape complex.
- **Talent and skills gaps:** This needs skills in data engineering, data science, domain knowledge and decision modeling to be successfully deployed. These hybrid skill sets are deficient in many organizations.
- **Model transparency and trust:** Explainability is becoming important as machine learning models grow more sophisticated. The decision-makers ought to have confidence and knowledge on the advice generated by DSS platforms
- **Change management and adoption:** Resistance to adoption may occur due to culture. Analytics have to be embedded in daily processes of decision making and this can only be achieved through leader sponsorship, training, and process redesign.

Companies that take the initiative to manage these obstacles are bound to achieve long term value.

3.5.8 Emerging Trends and Future Outlook

The Data Analytics and DSS are currently experiencing growth. The future of decision intelligence platform is being characterized by a few trends. The autonomous decision systems now appearing (made possible by the artificial intelligence and machine learning) can be constantly updated and adjusted. Data exploration is becoming simpler, with augmented analytics that have been designed to enable exploration with a natural language and automatic generation of information. In the actual sense of industrial and smart infrastructure, real-time decision support is expanding once the tools of the Internet of Things information are incorporated. Cloud-native architectures are making it easier to access and scale, and edge computing is reducing decision-latencies of time-constrained decisions. The other pattern is democratization of analytics. Low-code tools and self-service platforms allow business users and not required to be data professionals to contribute to making data-driven decisions. This sort of shift serves to encourage more agility of the organization, but it also leads to the increased focus on the problem of governance and data literacy.

The future will see the most successful business enterprises being the ones that view decision intelligence as a strategic resource to utilize as opposed to the adoption as a sterile technological application. The integration of Data Analytics and Decision Support System is among the most notable instances in the process of decision-making of an enterprise. Organizations can use raw data to create actionable information when it is needed through advanced analytics, user-friendly interfaces and data pipelines of mass data. The strategic payoff of this is noteworthy even though there exist current implementation problems that require attention particularly data quality, integration, and talent. As the level of digital transformation grows, DSS platforms built around analytics will become even more significant to the competitiveness of the enterprise. The best organizations that will succeed in harnessing the potential of intelligent decision support in the future will be those that make investments in scalable infrastructure, a sound governance system, and a data culture.

3.6 CYBERSECURITY AND ENTERPRISE RESILIENCE

The move of the digital transformation which currently holds the greater part of every society has turned cybersecurity into the key organizational defense mechanism that helps enterprises to defend against all threats. The risk of cyber-attacks has been on the rise as organizations start depending on their interdependent digital systems that are based on cloud computing technology, automated systems, and data analytics features. Companies should have fully integrated security frameworks that secure their activities since traditional security strategies can no longer secure their organizations against the current cyber threats. Cyber resilience is an integration of information security, business continuity management and risk assessment along with organizational adaptability to build a centralized structure of operation.

Cybersecurity resilience within organizations reflects how they are able to withstand an attack as well as manage and recover following devastating cyber-attacks. The entire picture is that digital systems have breaches as well as disruptions that cannot be avoided altogether. Digital businesses can reach the stage of maturity by being able to be ready to the events that destabilize the business and continue to provide basic services in such situations. The cybersecurity frameworks also demand organizations to establish cybersecurity and resilience practices as they establish their governance systems and operational systems on their digital projects.

3.6.1 Knowledge of Cyber Resilience.

Cyber resilience allows organizations to manage all the elements of cyber disruptions since it helps organizations to anticipate attacks, develop defensive mechanisms, operational continuity during an attack, as well as devising attack recovery mechanisms. The system integrates cybersecurity, business continuity management, disaster recovery and organizational risk management in a single structure. Cybersecurity should strengthen its protection strategies since the current cyber threats are surpassing the common security strategies as business activities must continue even after the cyber-attack has taken place.

The advanced capabilities of threat actors have made it necessary to adopt this complete understanding. Today, modern attackers have shifted their tactics to use human weaknesses and supply chain dependencies together with system misconfigurations and identity system flaws instead of depending on technical brute-force methods. Organizations must build their security systems around the possibility of breaches and they need to focus on quick threat identification together with danger control and system restoration.

Cyber resilience enables organizations to build digital trust which represents the confidence that stakeholders have in an organization's ability to protect data and keep services running while securing its essential resources. Organizations without this trust face three major challenges which include customer confidence loss and penalties from regulators and disruptions to their daily operations.

3.6.2 Strategic Importance for Digital Enterprises

Because businesses now view cyber threats as a direct threat to their financial performance which requires security solutions to protect their revenue streams Cyber threats have grown into a major business risk which requires organizations to adopt cyber resilience strategies. Digital platforms serve as essential components for generating revenue while maintaining customer relationships and managing supply chain operations and enhancing employee efficiency. The organization faces financial losses and reputation damage because of operational interruptions that last more than three hours.

The organizations that develop strong cyber resilience strategies will achieve these outcomes:

- They will continue providing essential services throughout every incident.
- They will decrease the financial losses and operational damage caused by security breaches.

- They will maintain their brand image while keeping their stakeholders safe.
- They will meet all regulatory requirements and stay prepared for audits.
- They will use new technologies with complete assurance.

Organizations that view cybersecurity as an essential business function will create better innovation pathways through secure security processes. Organizations which depend on security systems that lack integration and operate through a reactive response system will develop more technical debt which leads to control problems and slower response times for security incidents.

3.6.3 Risk-Based Cyber Resilience Strategy

The first step toward developing effective cyber protection measures requires organizations to use risk assessment methods that match their core business objectives. The development of security programs by advanced organizations requires them to identify essential business operations and digital systems and critical business assets. The security investments need to concentrate on testing areas which will produce maximum business interruption results because this method allows for security investment evaluation.

The implementation of a complete strategic plan requires organizations to use three distinct control methods. The purpose of preventive controls is to prevent incidents from occurring. Organizations implement a security program that includes secure configuration and vulnerability management and identity controls and network segmentation and employee awareness training programs.

The main goal of detective controls is to identify suspicious behavior in a quick manner. The security system uses continuous monitoring and behavioral analytics and threat intelligence integration and security analytics platforms as its primary components.

The organization can achieve quick incident control and system restoration through the application of corrective controls. The quick restoration of operations depends on incident response playbooks which enable automated remediation together with disaster recovery systems and business continuity plans.

The optimal control distribution is going to vary based on the requirements of each particular industry and regulatory framework and approach to risk management that involves organizations. The financial and healthcare sectors that work under stringent regulations require organizations to create safe and sophisticate preventive and inquisitive safety measures whereas digital native ones need to build the strength to recover and robust system structures.

3.6.4 Governance and Organizational Alignment

Cyber resilience is an area that requires effective governance system and collaboration among various departments besides technical skills. The top management needs to build effective accountability systems that will integrate cybersecurity goals and business performance. This report sets the protocols of data ownership identification and risk tolerance development and establishment of risk escalation processes and crisis communication planning.

An effective governance model typically incorporates:

- Board and executive oversight of cyber risk
- Enterprise risk management integration
- Clear roles across security, IT, legal, and operations
- Third-party and supply chain risk management
- Continuous compliance monitoring

Collaboration across the ecosystem is particularly important. Third-party vendors and software supply chains and partner integrations now serve as the primary sources for most cyber incidents. Enterprises must therefore extend resilience practices beyond organizational boundaries.

3.6.5 Standards and Frameworks Supporting Cyber Resilience

Organizations use best-practice frameworks to achieve cyber resilience because these frameworks deliver complete operational direction. The

Information Technology Infrastructure Library (ITIL) offers a service lifecycle approach that aligns security with service management. The ITIL framework defines resilience through its process to identify vital services which establishes protective measures for their secure operation and ongoing assessment and advancement. The lifecycle perspective ensures that other organizations use resilience as their core operational method instead of treating it as a separate security operation.

Another extensively used framework based on six fundamental functions is the NIST Identify, Protect, Detect, Respond, Recover, and Govern comprise the cybersecurity framework. The functions create a comprehensive model which includes policy elements and technical safeguards and monitoring systems and incident response protocols and recovery strategies. Most enterprises use NIST CSF to assess their current cyber security maturity level while developing plans for future improvements.

The security frameworks help organizations standardize their security operations through enterprise architecture practices while eliminating security control gaps and helping them meet regulatory requirements.

3.6.6 Essential Technologies for Cyber Resilience

Advanced security technologies which deliver visibility and automate processes while building up defense mechanisms serve as the main requirements for contemporary cyber resilience.

"Security information and event management" (SIEM) platforms use their capacity to collect and evaluate enterprise logs from all operational areas to create a unified system which detects possible security breaches. The combination of user and entity behavior analytics with SIEM solutions enables detection of unusual activities which traditional rule-based systems cannot identify.

Identity and access management (IAM) has become a foundational control layer as identity-based attacks continue to rise. Organizations implement three security measures which include strong authentication and least-privilege access controls together with lifecycle management processes to protect their critical resources from unauthorized access by users and services.

Zero-trust architecture functions as a new security framework which has developed from earlier security paradigms. Zero trust security systems require continuous verification of access requests, which applies to both identity information and device status and user environment. The model serves critical functions for organizations that operate with cloud-first and hybrid work environments.

Cloud security platforms enable organizations to guard their workloads which operate in both hybrid and multicloud environments through their specialized protection mechanisms. The tools provide solutions which protect against configuration-based threats while securing workloads and identifying threats that target cloud-native environments.

The resilience stack receives its final component through disaster recovery and continuous monitoring solutions which enable organizations to restore their operations rapidly while maintaining ongoing assessments of their security status.

3.6.7 Cyber Resilience in the Age of Artificial Intelligence

The nature of threats to security and the manner in which individuals defend themselves against the threats is being transformed by artificial intelligence. The AI security systems also detects abnormal activities as they apply their sophisticated detection framework alongside managing the threat evaluation activities and accelerating their reaction to security threats. Machine learning models are able to detect fine behavioral anomalies that would be difficult to detect at scale by human analysts. The appearance of artificial intelligence introduces new threats, which result in the development of new risks. Uncontrolled AI systems can reveal sensitive information, form shadow automation channels, or cause risks related to model manipulation. Advanced phishing attacks and deepfake attacks are created with the help of generative AI tools, and system vulnerabilities can be discovered using automated methods, as undertaken by cybercriminals.

The enterprises should, therefore, embrace balanced AI governance that incorporates: The nature of threats to security and the manner in which individuals defend themselves against the threats is being transformed by artificial intelligence. The AI security systems also detects abnormal activities as they apply their sophisticated detection framework alongside managing the threat evaluation activities and accelerating their reaction to security threats. Machine learning models are able to detect fine behavioral anomalies that would be difficult to detect at scale by human analysts. The appearance of artificial intelligence introduces new threats, which result in the development of new risks. Uncontrolled AI systems can reveal sensitive information, form shadow automation channels, or cause risks related to model manipulation. Advanced phishing attacks and deepfake attacks are created with the help of generative AI tools, and system vulnerabilities can be discovered using automated methods, as undertaken by cybercriminals.

Enterprises, therefore, should appreciate equal ways of AI governance:

- Strong access controls for AI systems
- Monitoring of model usage and outputs
- Secure data pipelines for training data
- Human oversight for high-risk decisions
- Alignment between AI strategy and cybersecurity policy

Organizations that successfully integrate AI into security operations achieve two benefits because their security systems can detect breaches faster while their security incidents become less damaging, which requires their governance systems to maintain their development advancements.

3.6.8 Operationalizing Enterprise Resilience

Organizations establish cyber resilience through their ongoing development of operational capabilities which requires continuous development work. Organizations create their enterprise architecture systems and DevSecOps pipelines and cloud governance structures and operating playbooks by implementing resilience strategies. Organizational core operational activities are performed in five major activities which comprise on-going risk assessment and threat hunting and red teaming exercises and tabletop simulations and post-incident learning loops. These are activities that organization undertakes to confirm their assumptions and identify the gaps in control and improve their responsiveness in the event of incidents. The human factor of the case is equally important. Security awareness training together with executive crisis preparedness training and cross-departmental incident response exercises drives actual resilience in organizations. Many significant data breaches have shown that organizations need both their technical security systems and their operational readiness to succeed in defense.

3.6.9 Future Outlook

The development of cyber resilience will proceed together with new technological innovations and changing threat patterns. The extended detection and response systems combine security data from various sources which include endpoints and networks and cloud workloads and identities to create a comprehensive solution for monitoring threats. Automation will take on the majority of basic tasks which involve equipment assessment and security containment so professionals can dedicate their time to investigating more difficult cases. Quantum computing creates both hazards and benefits for society. The technology will ultimately make current encryption systems less secure yet it also promotes the creation of quantum-safe cryptographic systems which will enhance future protection of sensitive data. The most resilient enterprises will establish cybersecurity as an adaptive business capability which uses intelligence to protect their operations. The ability of organizations to maintain credibility and operational security in a digital world will depend on their ability to create continuous learning systems which provide architectural flexibility through their strategic resource allocation methods.

Successful digital transformation requires organizations to integrate cybersecurity measures with their enterprise resilience strategies.

Businesses that integrate resilience into their technology framework and decision-making process and daily operations will achieve superior results when facing disruptions while safeguarding their stakeholder interests and maintaining their ability to innovate through changing cyber threats.

3.7 SUMMARY

Modern digital enterprises require fundamental cybersecurity and enterprise resilience capabilities as their essential operational foundations. The growing use of cloud platforms and intelligent automation and interconnected ecosystems has created heightened cybersecurity risks which now pose greater threats to organizations. The chapter demonstrated that organizations need to move beyond perimeter-based security measures because they now require complete cyber resilience solutions that encompass all security functions. Cybersecurity alignment with business continuity governance and risk management practices makes organizations stable in their operations. The organization implements its resilience framework through risk-based control models and zero-trust architecture and continuous monitoring systems.

The chapter described the ways in which organizations should implement advanced technologies through their adaptive defense systems by using AI-based security analytics and identity-centric control systems and cloud-native protection technologies. The paper found three major issues that organizations encounter with AI which include supply chain security risks and system vulnerabilities and the growing complexity of digital environments. Those organizations that create resilience based on its architectural design and the culture of foundation and decision-making processes will define their success in business in the future. The organizations developing combined system of cyber resilience will enjoy enhanced digital trust safeguards, along with business continuity and ability to innovate due to the rising threat landscape.

MULTIPLE CHOICE QUESTIONS (MCQS)

1. **What is the primary goal of digital technologies in enterprise transformation?**

   A. Reduce employee count

   B. Improve operational efficiency and innovation

   C. Eliminate legacy systems entirely

   D. Replace all human decision-making

2. **Which of the following best describes Artificial Intelligence (AI) in enterprises?**

   A. Manual data processing system

   B. Rule-based static programming

   C. Systems that simulate human intelligence for decision-making

   D. Hardware-only solutions

3. **Intelligent Automation is a combination of:**

   A. Hardware and networking

   B. AI and Robotic Process Automation (RPA)

   C. Databases and spreadsheets

   D. Manual and digital processes

4. **What is a key benefit of Cloud Computing for enterprises?**

   A. Increased capital expenditure

   B. Limited scalability

   C. On-demand resource availability

   D. Dependency on physical servers only

5. **Which cloud service model provides a platform for developers to build applications?**

   A. IaaS (Infrastructure as a Service)

   B. SaaS (Software as a Service)

   C. PaaS (Platform as a Service)

   D. DaaS (Data as a Service)

6. **The Internet of Things (IoT) primarily enables:**

   A. Manual data entry

   B. Connectivity between physical devices and digital systems

   C. Offline data storage

   D. Reduction in internet usage

7. **What is the main purpose of Data Analytics in enterprises?**

   A. Store data indefinitely

   B. Replace databases

   C. Extract insights for decision-making

   D. Eliminate human involvement

8. **Decision Support Systems (DSS) help organizations by:**

   A. Automating only hardware tasks

   B. Providing data-driven insights for decisions

   C. Eliminating leadership roles

   D. Storing unstructured data only

9. **Which of the following is a key component of Cybersecurity?**

   A. Ignoring threats

   B. Data encryption and threat detection

   C. Reducing system access for all users

   D. Avoiding cloud usage

10. **Enterprise resilience refers to:**
    A. Avoiding all digital technologies
    B. Ability to recover and adapt to disruptions
    C. Eliminating cybersecurity risks completely
    D. Reducing IT investments

Answers

1	2	3	4	5	6	7	8	9	10
B	C	B	C	C	B	C	B	B	C

Chapter 4
Transformation Execution and Change Management

4.1 OVERVIEW

The execution phase is the point of success or failure of digital transformation initiatives, which are implemented with a strategy being converted into a coordinated action of technology, processes, and people. Implementation of transformation is not a project but the curved and ongoing process which needs to be governed and strongly led by the leadership and should be delivered through adaptable delivery patterns. Companies need to stop the planning process and start to operationalize the change based on well-defined roadmaps, quantifiable results, and cross-functional cooperation. At this point, the attention changes to how to transform effectively and sustainably rather than the question of what to transform.

Change management is a key component in making sure that the transformation efforts are embraced, escalated and integrated into the day-to-day activities. The greatest obstacles usually involve resistance to change, skill deficits, old ways of thinking, and silo thinking, rather than technology. Thus, effective organizations combine the principle of change management with agile implementation, risk management, and workforce empowerment. The chapter analyzes the essential elements needed to effectively implement transformation initiatives, which are governance and risk management, Agile and DevOps adoption, business process modernization, organizational capability building, and ecosystem collaboration. Collectively, these aspects combine into a unified implementation model which helps organizations to achieve value at a quicker pace and still control, comply and remain strategic.

4.2 GOVERNANCE AND RISK MANAGEMENT

Digital transformation governance functions as the institutional framework that connects innovation efforts with business objectives while maintaining operational requirements and legal standards. Modern enterprises require governance to function as an operational framework that enables organizations to achieve fast expansion while creating business value. Organizations need governance to establish decision-making frameworks and financial management procedures and technical limits when they implement cloud-native platforms and intelligent automation and data-driven business models. Organizations achieve better results through effective governance because it enables them to allocate transformation resources based on their strategic importance and potential danger, which helps them to avoid technology waste and unsupervised technical debt. Organizations that develop governance as an evolving capability will achieve better results when they need to handle digital changes and respond to unexpected market changes (vegam.ai, 2025).

4.2.1 Evolution from Traditional IT Governance to Digital Governance

Traditional IT governance emerged during a period that featured technological environments that maintained stability and software development processes that took extended periods to complete. The system required organizations to control operations from a central point while they created future plans through yearly procedures and approved project milestones to safeguard their business operations. The requirement for digital transformation to deliver software at all times and test new ideas and work together across different teams shows how current governance systems do not support these needs. Digital governance in the present day has changed its approach to management by moving away from project-based supervision toward product and platform administration. Organizations now delegate decision-making powers to teams that operate according to their established rules. Organizations now use automated systems to manage compliance and risk controls, which operate during their delivery processes to provide constant monitoring instead of needing standard audit procedures. The current transformation shows a complete institutional change from traditional command systems toward flexible management practices that use data to enhance both innovation capacity and organizational resilience.

4.2.2 Governance Operating Models

Enterprises establish their governance systems through operational frameworks which determine decision-making processes and establish responsibilities while creating methods to enforce regulations. A centralized governance model concentrates decision authority at the enterprise level and is often associated with strong standardization and regulatory control. The system decreases technology distribution problems and makes it easier to follow regulations but it prevents quick technological development and creates delays because of the mandatory approval process. Federated governance enables business units to control their operational activities while the organization maintains its core policies and common resources. Organizations in the digital age select this framework because it maintains operational flexibility while maintaining business continuity. The governance model allows product teams to operate independently through its complete decentralization which enables them to test new ideas while keeping strong connections to business objectives. The absence of effective automated control mechanisms results in decentralization which causes organizations to experience operational breakdowns and security problems and data management issues. Most large enterprises choose federated operating structures because these systems provide executives with strategic authority while allowing local business units to operate with independent decision-making power.

4.2.3 Core Governance Domains

Digital governance needs to operate across different areas which work together to protect business integrity. Strategic and portfolio governance connects digital investments to the business requirements and evaluates the benefits acquired under the transformation projects. Architecture governance maintains technical coherence by enforcing reference architectures and technology standards and design review practices which reduce technical debt and increase platform reuse. Organizations depend on advanced analytics and AI so data governance has become critical to establish who owns data assets and set quality requirements and privacy regulations and data asset management procedures. Security and compliance governance protects organizations from increasing cyber threats by combining identity management with vulnerability monitoring and compliance assessment for their continuous delivery systems. Vendor and ecosystem governance protects organizations from cloud provider and SaaS platform and strategic partner risks by controlling third-party dependencies which lead to dangerous exposure. The governance domains work together to establish a complete control framework which enables organizations to expand their digital operations.

4.2.4 Risk Management in Digital Transformation

Digital transformation makes it possible to create additional security threats which organizations must control. The risk of system failures increases because organizations now use interconnected systems which depend on real-time platforms to deliver customer services. The integration of various technologies creates cybersecurity threats because organizations must manage their complex relationships between their old systems and new systems, yet their security problems increase because APIs and cloud services and remote access models create additional entry points for attackers. Automated systems create operational dangers because their full-scale operation fails, and strict data protection laws create higher risks for data breaches. Transformation programs encounter two major adoption obstacles because employees and customers refuse to accept new work methods, while organizations depend heavily on outside vendors, which creates third-party risks. An organization needs to assess all aspects of its transformation process by including both its technical systems and its organizational structure.

4.2.5 From Periodic Risk Reviews to Continuous Risk Management

The risk management system relied on three main components, which included periodic assessments and manual testing procedures, and fixed risk registers as its foundational elements. The current strategy is effective in those settings that have gradual changes and does not suit the needs of digital companies with continuous system upgrades and instant customer support. Continuous risk management systems that are used in organizations in the contemporary world are embraced in the organizations due to their ability to allow the organization to monitor risks and control its effectiveness in real time. The system makes use of automated monitoring tools that collect telemetry data of applications and infrastructural systems and user activities, which assists in detecting abnormalities at an early stage. Embedded compliance checks can be used by development teams, which are compatible with their development pipelines, and executives can view risk dashboards indicating the current risk information. The organization uses predictive analytics along with scenario modelling to enhance its ability to detect future disruptions. The new approach transforms the risk management to an active intelligence-based process, as opposed to a passive auditing, and thus allows rapid and safe development of innovations.

4.2.6 Integrating Risk Management with Agile and DevOps

The most prominent development in digital governance studies is provided by the organizations that join the risk management procedures with their agile development operations and DevOps operational practices. The conventional security control and compliance requirement of the systems acted as last lines of defense which led to delays in the operation processes and consequently increased the product development cycle. DevSecops practices applied by modern enterprises define security and privacy protection and compliance requirements and make them integral elements of software development processes.

The team employs the shift-left testing and automated vulnerability scanning and infrastructure-as-code validation and policy-as-code enforcement to find and address security threats in earlier stages of the project. The system generates full audit trails as it automatically gathers data that assists the organizations to comply with the regulatory requirements without sluggishness of their operations. Responsible product teams will provide a risk management system that will help to make governance an accountability, rather than a bureaucratic process which is stopped in red tape.

4.2.7 Risk Quantification and Prioritization

The first step that organizations have to take to reduce the various risks associated with digital transformation is to identify their core business functions. Organisations employ quantitative risk assessment methods to reposition their decisions and decisions based on progressive business practices. The organizations can find the locations with a risk exposure that are high by integrating the risk scoring models, heat maps, and scenario analysis. In addition to that, business impact analysis associates the technical risks with their impacts on revenue, customer experience, and business continuity. Organizations employ probabilistic methods such as Monte Carlo simulation to assess the extent of their potential financial losses. By assessing risk either in financial terms or customer impact metrics, the leadership teams gain the capability to make wiser investment decisions while at the same time reshaping their resource allocation. The analytical technique provides the means for the organizations to practice risk, based governance where they tailor the risk control measures to the specific risk exposure levels of their business instead of simply running standard control procedures.

4.2.8 Governance Metrics and Performance Monitoring

The effectiveness and credibility of governance systems depends on their ability to establish measurable standards. Organizations that lead their industries create performance metrics which measure their ability to control operations and their capacity to deliver products. The digital ecosystem health assessment uses deployment frequency and change failure rate and mean time to detect and respond to incidents and policy compliance rates and data quality scores as metrics. The organization uses vendor performance indicators together with audit remediation timelines to establish stronger control mechanisms for managing external dependencies. Executives and risk leaders use real-time dashboards to track trends through continuous monitoring instead of using historical reports. The governance metrics need to establish a balance because their current state provides incentives for organizations to practice excessive caution which slows down their innovation processes. Creating a Future-Ready Governance Model.

Companies that are planning ahead are embracing systems of governance that emphasize on permeable organizational boundaries rather than security gateways. The technique implements automatic policies that set limits of operations within teams to perform their tasks. The system keeps track of operations on-going rather than applying scheduled assessments with product-based accountability ensuring that risk management occurs at the delivery point. The data insights enable organizations to make investment decisions and manage their operations which they attain through ecosystem-conscious governance that manages their growing network of partners and platform relationships. The most mature organizations also do not consider governance as a constraint but rather a strategic competence that creates trust among customers, regulators and stakeholders. Automation and analytics are combined with cultural alignment that will allow enterprises to attain their objectives of rapid innovation and proper risk management.

Digital transformation requires both governance functions and risk management functions in order to attain its objectives. The contemporary business entity needs to adapt to the strict, centralized management and control towards the adaptive, automated, and monitored control setting. Federated governance models can deliver the best balance between agility and standardization, whereas DevSecOps do incorporate risk controls directly into delivery pipelines. Continuous risk monitoring is applied in conjunction with quantitative prioritization techniques and real-time performance indicators to manage the growing digital risk fronts in organizations. By updating their governance systems with technological and operation changes, enterprises will benefit and can sustain their digital value to remain resilient and compliant and stay trusted by their stakeholders. The company is also seeking to get quick developments whilst ensuring great operational reliability.

4.2.9 Common Pitfalls and Anti-Patterns

The fact that people are aware of the need to change has not helped the organizations modernize their governance systems. The burden of bureaucracy in organizations has posed a universal threat since organizations have too many steps of approval and handwriting checks that lead to a slow delivery of services and more illegal use of IT. Teams perceive compliance as an obstacle that cannot allow the organization to move forward since organizations do not associate the governance processes and business value. The two barriers confront organizations since their manual spreadsheet controls fail to work with cloud-native settings and their individual risk management systems introduce security gaps in organizations. Various business entities have different standards and this poses a challenge to security as well as system interoperability. Lack of executive support and funding of automation puts barriers that make governance modernization projects not to prosper. The organizations should identify and rectify these anti-patterns as this aids them in continuing on the transformation journey.

4.2.10 Building a Future-Ready Governance Model

Companies that are planning ahead are embracing systems of governance that emphasize on permeable organizational boundaries rather than security gateways. The technique implements automatic policies that set limits of operations within teams to perform their tasks. The system keeps track of operations on-going rather than applying scheduled assessments with product-based accountability ensuring that risk management occurs at the delivery point. The data insights enable organizations to make investment decisions and manage their operations which they attain through ecosystem-conscious governance that manages their growing network of partners and platform relationships. The most mature organizations also do not consider governance as a constraint but rather a strategic competence that creates trust among customers, regulators and stakeholders. Automation and analytics are combined with cultural alignment that will allow enterprises to attain their objectives of rapid innovation and proper risk management.

Digital transformation requires both governance functions and risk management functions in order to attain its objectives. The contemporary business entity needs to adapt to the strict, centralized management and control towards the adaptive, automated, and monitored control setting. Federated governance models can deliver the best balance between agility and standardization, whereas DevSecOps do incorporate risk controls directly into delivery pipelines. Continuous risk monitoring is applied in conjunction with quantitative prioritization techniques and real-time performance indicators to manage the growing digital risk fronts in organizations. By updating their governance systems with technological and operation changes, enterprises will benefit and can sustain their digital value to remain resilient and compliant and stay trusted by their stakeholders.

4.3 AGILE AND DEVOPS ADOPTION

Digital transformation success now depends on organizations using Agile and DevOps as their main operational framework. The traditional software delivery models, which depend on extended-release periods and separate operational groups and fixed procedures for changes, fail to meet the requirements of the current digital economy, which needs rapid customer service. Organizations need to develop new features at high speed while they keep their systems protected and operational and their products secure. The combination of Agile and DevOps provides organizations with their essential operational framework and their necessary engineering methods to reach their goals (Buchanan, 2025).

Agile enables teams to create their work plans more effectively while delivering value to their customers through iterative processes. DevOps extends this approach to all software development phases because it combines development work with operational tasks and security needs and quality engineering functions. The implementation of Agile and DevOps lets organizations transition their work approach from project-based delivery methods to product-based development of digital platforms that undergo constant improvement.

4.3.1 Strategic Importance of Agile in Digital Transformation

The Agile methodologies developed to solve waterfall development problems because waterfall development failed to deal with shifting project needs and customer wants. The digital transformation process uses Agile as its project management method which also serves as the foundation for organizations to adopt customer-centric approaches that support quick testing and flexible project management. The transformation process enables organizations to execute their large-scale changes through Agile which organizes work into small parts that create tangible results for their business. The method of incremental delivery decreases delivery risks while it increases stakeholder awareness and it speeds up the feedback process between users and development teams. As digital products become the main factor that determines market competition, Agile practices enable businesses to synchronize their technology delivery with their changing business requirements.

Agile promotes innovation through its support of cross-departmental teamwork, ongoing education, and the process of making incremental advancements. The Agile system helps teams develop better abilities which enable them to manage the unpredictable nature of digital transformation projects that use emerging technologies like artificial intelligence and cloud-native platforms and advanced analytics.

4.3.2 Core Principles of Agile Adoption

- **Customer value as the primary focus:** Agile directs its work because it needs to provide customers with valuable results more than completing its technical tasks. The team needs to investigate user requirements to create features that enhance both customer experience and system usability and business results. The value-first approach maintains development work at the correct path because it matches market requirements and strategic business objectives.
- **Early and frequent delivery of working software:** Agile requires teams to deliver usable software increments through short development cycles instead of waiting for their next major software release. Organizations achieve benefits earlier because they can use

continuous delivery to decrease risks and obtain quicker feedback. The system enables stakeholders to assess progress while they modify their focus according to actual results, not estimated results.

- **Embracing change as a competitive advantage:** Agile frameworks handle requirement changes because they accept that all changes will occur while some changes actually bring value. The development team needs to build their structure, which enables them to adapt to new business requirements and customer feedback and market changes, which can happen during any project phase. Organizations need this ability to adjust because digital transformation creates continuous uncertainty together with ongoing technological progress.
- **Cross-functional, stable team structures:** Agile organizations create permanent teams which unite diverse professionals to deliver complete value through their cross-functional expertise. Product teams usually consist of product owners who work with developers and testers and UX designers and operations or platform specialists. Teams that operate continuously acquire expertise about their domain while they work together, which decreases the time needed for handoffs and, therefore, leads to better productivity and work results.
- **Short, time-boxed iterations (sprints):** Work is organized into fixed-duration cycles—commonly two to four weeks—known as sprints. In a sprint, teams organize priorities and create features, conduct tests, and present a working software. Time-boxing establishes a predictable delivery pace, enhances concentration, and allows a high frequency of inspection and process and product adaptation.
- **Continuous stakeholder engagement and feedback loops:** Agile is based on frequent responses of the business stakeholders, customers, and end users. Sprint reviews, demos, and backlog refinement sessions help to make sure that the delivered features are up to the expectations and make them sustainable to the business goals. Constant feedback minimizes the possibility of creating the wrong solution and enhances business-IT alignment.

- **Outcome-based performance measurement:** Agile redirects the emphasis of the traditional output metrics, e.g., lines of code, the number of tasks completed or the number of hours worked, to outcome-based metrics. Customer satisfaction, business value delivered, feature adoption and time-to-value are important indicators. This change supports Agile as a business transformation facilitator, but not a development practice.
- **Incremental and iterative development approach:** Agile advocates the creation of solutions in small steps rather than trying to do big releases. With every iteration, functional value is introduced which can be tested, validated and enhanced. This method minimizes technical and business risk and allows learning to occur at a quicker pace and correcting of courses.
- **Close collaboration between business and technology teams:** Agile dismantles the traditional silos due to the fostering of daily communication between product owners and the business stakeholders as well as the engineering teams. The common ownership of priorities and results guarantees that delivery of technology is closely related to business strategy and customers.
- **Work transparency and visibility**: Agile teams have visible backlogs, sprint boards and progress metrics that enable stakeholders to monitor status up to date. This openness fosters trust, aids in making decisions using data, and allows promptly discovering risks or bottlenecks.
- **Perspective-driven continuous improvement:** Teams carry out retrospectives at the end of every sprint to review what was good and what was bad and how things can be done better. This inbuilt learning loop creates an atmosphere of trial and error, responsibility and operational superiority in the long run.
- **Independent and self-managed teams:** Agile facilitates teams to decide daily deliveries within a specific scope of strategy. Empowerment enhances ownership, enhances speed in problem solving and team motivation. Leadership changes its directive control to enabling and coaching.

- **Slow rate of delivery:** Agile focuses on the need to consistently sustain a work rhythm and avoids both periodic overtime and crisis-based releases. Sustainable pace enhances the sustainability of productivity, burnout and quality of products.
- **Built-in quality mindset:** Quality is not considered an independent phase but it is integrated throughout the lifecycle of development. Automation of tests, continuous integration and definition of done are practices that make sure that every increment is released at agreed quality levels.
- **Congruence with overall digital transformation objectives:** Finally, the adoption of Agile promotes the enterprise change by facilitating quicker innovation, enhanced responsiveness to market shifts, and closer interconnection of technology investment and business results. The organizations that internalize these principles take the next step of being Agile at scale by not only doing Agile.

4.3.3 Scaling Agile Across the Enterprise

The organization initially enters its Agile structure by having a team implementation before it experiences trouble in its expansion of its system to large scale and complex business processes. The Agile framework implementation process requires organizations to change their system of funds and mode of governance and business processes. On the program level, several Agile teams will need to align themselves based on a common set of goals and architectural dependencies and release planning. The organization deploys the systematic strategies of scaling operations that generate product-based value chain. The portfolio-level agility system extends Agile principles throughout investment planning because it transitions funding from temporary projects to permanent product teams that deliver ongoing value. The implementation of Enterprise Agile requires business units to establish operational connections with their IT departments. The development process uses collaborative workflows to replace traditional handoff methods which separate requirements from development and testing and operations. The leadership team performs essential functions by eliminating organizational obstacles and establishing new performance rewards and creating a workplace environment that encourages innovation and knowledge development.

4.3.4 DevOps as an Extension of Agile

Agile improves planning and development practices, but it fails to provide complete solutions for all digital system deployment and operational challenges which emerge during their entire system lifecycle. The DevOps methodology was created to solve this problem by merging development work with operational work into a single automated system for delivering software. DevOps enables organizations to develop and deliver products through continuous software integration and delivery which includes automated infrastructure management and instant system performance assessment. Digital transformation initiatives require DevOps implementation to enable organizations to build cloud-native systems and operate microservices architectures and utilize platform-based business models. Through automatic task execution and the removal of manual work processes DevOps achieves faster operational cycles while decreasing the likelihood of human mistakes. The solution helps team members who previously worked independently to work together better because they now share responsibility for system performance and customer satisfaction.

4.3.5 Core DevOps Capabilities

An advanced DevOps environment needs to establish multiple basic elements. The process of Continuous integration establishes automatic building and testing of code changes whenever developers make their updates which helps teams find defects at an early stage. The Continuous delivery and deployment pipelines of software production enable automatic software releases which protect the security of production systems during their deployment process.

Teams use Infrastructure as Code (IaC) to create and operate built environments through scripts that use version control to enhance their infrastructure operations. The automated testing frameworks provide quality assurance support which covers unit testing, integration testing and performance testing activities. Monitoring and observability tools provide organizations with immediate system health information and user activity data and details about potential operational threats.

The combination of these capabilities establishes an environment that enables fast software delivery with minimal operational risks while supporting ongoing product development.

4.3.6 Cultural Transformation and DevOps Mindset

The main obstacle in organizations which adopt Agile and DevOps methods stems from their organizational culture instead of any technical problems. Organizations start by implementing tools and automation but they fail to recognize that developing a new mindset requires both behavioral alterations and procedural changes.

DevOps requires organizations to shift from siloed accountability systems which restrict responsibility to a system which enables all members to share accountability for project outcomes. Development teams must assume responsibility for all aspects of production performance while operations teams need to become full partners who help organizations achieve speedy modifications.The cultural unification process reaches its peak when people follow the principle that states "you build it, you run it" because it leads to system ownership.

Organizations require three cultural elements which include psychological safety, blameless postmortems and continuous learning. Organizations need to move beyond traditional change approval processes which use strict standards toward adopting systems which deliver automated risk-based controls that permit fast product development while maintaining operational stability.

The process of organizational change needs strong leadership backing to succeed. The absence of executive backing, together with misaligned incentive structures, prevents organizations from successfully implementing their Agile and DevOps initiatives beyond their initial experimental phase.

4.3.7 Integrating Security: The Rise of DevSecOps

The delivery pipelines directly require the integration of security and compliance for faster release velocity. DevSecOps takes DevOps a step further by embedding security throughout the software development lifecycle. The main features of DevSecOps are implemented through automated vulnerability scanning alongside checking dependencies, container security, and secrets management, and policy, as, code enforcement.

By implementing security tests at the earlier stages of the development process, the security vulnerabilities costs and their operational impacts can be reduced. Companies can comply with regulations through continuous monitoring without losing their operational efficiency. By implementing the division of security responsibilities among the teams, DevSecOps is capable of resolving the conflict between operational efficiency and security governance that already existed. The company becomes less vulnerable to cyber-attacks, which are intensifying nowadays.

4.3.8 Measuring Agile and DevOps Performance

Organizations need to create significant performance metrics which will measure both their delivery speed and operational efficiency to maintain their ongoing progress. Digital organizations achieve their best results through monitoring four key metrics which include deployment frequency and lead time for changes and change failure rate and mean time to recover from incidents. The two metrics provide organizations with complete understanding of their operational speed and system reliability. Engineering output measurement through additional metrics which include customer satisfaction and feature adoption rates and business value delivered enables organizations to achieve their strategic goals. The use of real-time dashboards together with automated data collection systems establishes transparent operations while enabling organizations to improve their processes. Metrics should guide learning processes because they help teams develop but teams should not face penalties due to their performance metrics. Organizations face risks when performance metrics get used improperly because it creates a need for employees to avoid risks which prevents them from achieving Agile and DevOps goals.

4.3.9 Common Challenges in Adoption

The organizations face difficulties in adopting Agile and DevOps despite their high demand from customers. The existing organizational systems create functional barriers that prevent different teams from working together. The pipeline adoption process gets delayed because of two factors, which include insufficient automation and technical debt. The continuous delivery system needs manual approval to operate, which creates a conflict with its governance model.

Organizations face major challenges because they lack sufficient skills in cloud engineering and automation and product management. Organizations that implement Agile ceremonies without understanding their core principles create an "Agile in name only" process. The process of adopting new methods becomes more difficult because these environments resist any changes to their established culture.

The organization requires a comprehensive solution that needs to create new operating models and establish leadership consensus and develop employee skills through training and execute plans through step-by-step methods.

4.3.10 Best Practices for Successful Adoption

Successful organizations that maintain their success through Agile and DevOps face several operational challenges which require them to execute best practices. Their operations start with established procedures which define their value streams and the responsibilities of their product owners. The team establishes automatic systems to expedite work processes by eliminating all manual tasks. Platform engineering departments develop common tools and foundational systems which help product development teams implement their work more efficiently.

Organizations develop essential abilities through continuous education initiatives and professional development groups which also enable knowledge exchange. Organizations now use updated governance frameworks which replace rigid approval processes with risk-based control systems. Successful enterprises use Agile and

DevOps as their permanent framework which builds organizational capacity through time instead of using them as temporary operational improvements.

Digital transformation needs organizations to adopt Agile and DevOps because they serve as essential components for successful large-scale implementation. The Agile framework establishes operational principles which enable organizations to deliver products through customer-focused iterative processes while DevOps provides the systems and cultural framework which supports ongoing system updates and dependable system maintenance. The two systems create a new operational model which drives organizations to adopt continuous delivery methods based on product development instead of traditional project management techniques.

Organizations need to develop their business by understanding three important elements which are their existing tools, their operational methods, and their need to create new governance processes, which guide their business development. Organizations achieve success through three essential elements which include implementing security through DevSecOps and creating performance metrics and removing organizational obstacles. Institutions that develop their Agile and DevOps capabilities through systematic implementation gain the capability to create products at high speed which meet evolving market demands while maintaining continuous digital output.

4.4 BUSINESS PROCESS MODERNIZATION

Digital transformation relies on business process modernization which creates a base for organizations to redesign their operational procedures and enhance their operational flexibility and productivity while delivering better results to their stakeholders. The core functions of many organizations developed through multiple small improvements which created disconnected work processes that required physical handovers and had duplicate checking procedures and limited tracking abilities between different stages of the production process. Organizations face innovation barriers because their existing methods restrict them which also creates delays in making decisions and raises their risk of operational failures. Organizations use modernization to completely change their work processes through digital technologies and data analysis and human-centered design methods (Harish, 2025).

Business process modernization requires complete process redesign whereas simple process automation only digitizes current business operations. It removes activities that do not create value while changing the fundamental foundations of work processes to fit modern business requirements and customer needs. Process transformation enables enterprises to realize business benefits from their technology investments through enterprise platform modernization.

4.4.1 Concept and Scope of Business Process Modernization

The term business process modernization describes the methodical change of corporate processes which results in improved operational agility and advanced decision-making capabilities and expanded organizational capacity and enhanced service delivery to customers. The method includes five components which are process redesign and workflow digitization and intelligent automation and real-time analytics and continuous optimization. The organization handles all aspects of its operations from front-office activities to middle-office tasks and back-office functions which include customer onboarding and order management and claims processing and supply chain activities and finance operations and human resource tasks.

Modernization efforts typically choose multiple strategic goals as their target. The first objective targets better customer and employee experiences through decreased friction and shorter operational times. The second objective establishes operational resilience through processes which can adjust to new circumstances. The third objective enhances decision-making through analytics which are integrated into the system and artificial intelligence-based insights. The system enables organizations to control their expenses through automatic process operation which minimizes human work and decreases mistakes.

The process of process modernization operates as an ongoing function which continues after the initial implementation. Organizations need to update their operational procedures because market dynamics and technological advancements and legal frameworks continuously change.

4.4.2 Drivers of Business Process Modernization

Organizations need to update their business processes because multiple forces create this necessity. The main factor driving this change is the increased demands from customers. Digital-native customers expect businesses to provide them with uninterrupted delivery of personalized services across multiple touchpoints. The existing systems which were built for batch processing and manual checks cannot fulfill these customer demands.

The market requires businesses to compete against their rivals. Organizations across all sectors use automation and AI with cloud platforms to boost their operational performance through enhanced process efficiency. Those who do not modernize their enterprises will find it easy to be overtaken by other competitors who are more nimble.

The organizations require updating of their systems due to operation difficulties. A large number of organizations conduct their business using their computers.

several isolated systems, and this leads to redundancy of work processes and it leads to various data management procedures. These faults in operation expose the organization to more risk besides more costs incurred by the organization. Modernization of processes assists organizations to provide standardized processes which facilitate operations control in a better manner.

It is a requirement that organizations change their operations due to the dual demands. The new digital systems provide organizations with improved capabilities for auditing their operations while tracking their processes and maintaining control over their activities, unlike previous manual systems. The present workforce trends, which include constant remote work and skill shortages, together with the need for organizations to create more complex positions, push businesses to implement automation for basic duties while they develop work systems that optimize human capacities.

4.4.3 Core Elements of Business Process Modernization

Successful business process modernization typically rests on three interconnected pillars.

A. **Human-centric experience design:** Current business operations develop their procedures according to the requirements of their customers and staff members and business associates. Human-centric process design uses methods that support both accessibility and user-friendly design and journey optimization. The organization uses customer journey mapping and service blueprinting and design thinking methods to discover operational challenges and create new ways of working. The project aims to develop user-friendly digital experiences that require minimal user effort while increasing user satisfaction.

B. **Agile and resilient operational backbone:** The operational backbone provides flexible functions which enable processes to grow and adapt while recovering from disruptions. The system base of this organization operates through cloud-native platforms together with API-based connections and its modular microservices and event-driven systems. Automated processes and real time tracking and self-recovery systems make the system more resilient since humans are not required to control the system. Companies that have robust operational foundations are able to provide new functionality in a short period and react efficiently to changes in the market.

C. **Data-driven process intelligence:** he operational processes currently being in operation give out a lot of operational data that can be analyzed to improve performance. Process mining, advanced analytics and artificial intelligence can be combined to help organizations comprehend their process flows in addition to identifying their bottlenecks in operations and variability in their processes. Predictive and prescriptive analytics allow organizations to make proactive decisions that help them to streamline their operations at all times. The dynamic adaptive systems which are developed by the active operational insight engine convert the workflow into learning processes.

4.4.4 Significant Technologies that make the processes modern

Technology is very essential in facilitating process transformation, but it has to be implemented in a good process structure.

- **Process mining and process discovery:** Process mining tools can also be used to develop actual process flow by analyzing the event logs of the system. This gives objective insight into the actual performance of work, which can be an eye opener in the existence of unknown bottlenecks, rework cycles, and compliance nonconformity. Organizations utilize such insights to focus on redesign efforts and gauge improvement.
- **Robotic Process Automation (RPA):** RPA automates rule-based repetitive tasks that had to be performed manually in the past. It comes in handy especially during high-volume back-office procedures like data entry, reconciliation and report generation. Although RPA is able to provide quick wins, it can work best through extending process redesign.
- **Intelligent automation and AI:** Artificial intelligence can go beyond basic rules associated with automation by providing document comprehension, predictive decision-making, and chatbots. Machine learning models are able to identify abnormalities, predict demand, and optimize routes in workflows. More flexible and self-enhancing processes are supported by intelligent automation.
- **Workflow orchestration platforms:** The modern workflow engines orchestrate system, team, and bot tasks. These offer a visibility, exception management and end-to-end control over business processes that are complex. Connection to APIs and microservices makes real-time process execution a possibility.

- **Cloud and integration platforms:** Cloud infrastructure offers scalability and flexibility needed in the modern processes. The integration platforms and APIs do bridge the once isolated systems, and the data flow throughout the enterprise ecosystem becomes smooth.

Process Modernization Lifecycle

A modernization of the business processes usually takes a systematic lifecycle. The process begins with the organizations undertaking process discovery and assessment in order to develop a workflow that reveals the existing operations and reveals their key issues besides determining their performance shortcomings. The stage involves the process mining and stakeholder interviews in order to gather process information in different sources. The second stage is process redesign which is the removal of processes that are not valuable and simplifies decision-making processes using digital tools by the teams. People-centered design methods make new working processes enhance user experience. The stage of automation and implementation presents the implementation of enabling technologies into the system with the introduction of RPA and AI and workflow platforms. The system builds integration with all the enterprise systems and data sources. Organizations embark on their post deployment work with the observation of performance and subsequent improvement. The system incorporates real-time analytics along with process intelligence tools to track the performance and locate issues which become the driver of continual improvements. Established organizations have a permanent practice of process improvement that ensures that modernization is a permanent feature of its business activity rather than a project-based activity.

4.4.5 Business Benefits of Process Modernization

Executing business process modernization correctly enables organizations to achieve significant benefits. Organizations experience better stakeholder satisfaction because their processes operate at higher speed and greater transparency and easier accessibility. The company has reduced customer onboarding times while improving service response times and making employee tasks lighter. Better process visibility allows organizations to create new service models and customized products while increasing their operational efficiency. Companies can use enhanced agility to expand their market presence because they can enter markets faster than their competitors. Companies attain better operational performance through shorter cycle times and decreased error rates and improved resource allocation. Organizations achieve cost savings through automation which decreases manual tasks and enables them to manage expenses during operational expansion. Organizations achieve better business intelligence through process modernization. Digital workflows that operate between all system components produce accurate data which enables predictive analytics and sound decision-making. Employee productivity rises because staff members move from basic duties to their new roles in data analysis and client interactions. Organizations achieve better compliance through automated controls which also boost their ability to prepare for audits.

4.4.6 Organizational and Cultural Implications

The modernization process requires organizations to undergo major changes that go beyond technological upgrades. The traditional functional silos of organizations create obstacles that prevent the implementation of end-to-end process management. Enterprises must therefore implement cross-functional governance together with product-based operating systems. The development of automation technology leads to changes in workforce roles, which automate repetitive tasks. Employees require training in data literacy, digital tools and process management skills. Organizations must use change management programs to overcome resistance and drive the successful implementation of new initiatives.

The commitment of leadership to a specific cause determines its ultimate outcome. Senior executives must show their commitment to strategic goals by providing funding while they establish a workplace culture that supports ongoing improvement through testing new ideas.

4.4.7 Risks and Challenges

- Over-automation without proper process redesign may simply accelerate inefficient workflows.

- Integration complexity between legacy and modern systems can delay expected benefits.
- Data quality issues can undermine the effectiveness of AI-driven decision-making.
- Insufficient change management may result in low user adoption and resistance.
- Greater the interconnectivity of the processes, the security vulnerability can be adopted.
- The risks of compliance increase with the increase in data flows between systems and partners.
- Fast modernization in the absence of architectural discipline may result in permanent turmoil.
- Organizations should strike a balance between fastness and good governance and good architecture.

4.4.8 Best Practices for Successful Modernization

Best companies have a number of practices that they embrace to achieve the highest success. They start by having clear business results as opposed to technology first thinking. Process discovery is also a data-based process, and process mining is frequently seen to create a factual base.

High-impact processes that influence customer experience or cost of operation are prioritized by the enterprises. Process simplification is conducted with the application of automation but not instead of it. Scalability is enhanced using platform based architectures and reusable components.

There is a high level of executive sponsorship and cross-functional cooperation which provides business and IT alignment. Constant feedback and monitoring contribute to continuous optimization. Lastly, organizations invest in long term transformation by building workforce capability.

4.4.9 Future Trends in Business Process Modernization

The upcoming process modernization wave will be driven by Hyperautomation, generative AI and autonomous operations. The processes now operate through event-driven systems which optimize themselves automatically. Business users can now design workflows through process innovation, which low-code and no-code platforms provide. Process intelligence platforms are developing into predictive control towers that display real-time operational data throughout the entire organization. Human–AI collaboration models will create new pathways for decisions to be made within workflows. The expansion of ecosystems will lead organizations to adopt inter-organizational process orchestration as a vital element for building their competitive edge.

The organizations which establish flexible data-based operational systems today will gain advantages from upcoming technological advancements.

Business process modernization is essential for enterprises seeking to become agile, resilient, and customer-centric in the digital era. The process requires complete workflow transformation through automation and analytics and cloud-based platform systems. Organizations achieve successful modernization through the combination of human-centered design, adaptable operational framework, and data-based intelligence system.

The organization gains three advantages through improved efficiency and better stakeholder experiences and increased business flexibility, but it must handle three challenges, which include cultural transformation and integration difficulties and governance threats. Core business transformation allows enterprises to attain operational excellence by implementing a lifecycle process and taking advantage of enabling technologies in the quest to achieve constant improvement.

4.5 ORGANIZATIONAL CHANGE AND SKILLS TRANSFORMATION

With the growing pace of organizations adopting Artificial Intelligence (AI) into the workflows of its primary business processes, including predictive analytics in the financial department and intelligent automation in supply chains, it has become clear that it is not only technological capability, which defines success. The real point of distinction is the effectiveness with which organizations can handle the human aspect of change. The use of AI is not a simple upgrade of the systems but a complete restructuring of the way work is done, decisions are made and value is generated. In that regard, Organizational Change Management (OCM) and workforce skills transformation become the mission-critical capabilities (Proctor, 2025).

The AI projects that do not consider the human factor are often met with opposition, lack of utilization and incomplete results. On the other hand, companies investing in a systematic change management approach and considering the possible ability development are much more likely to attain sustainable change. Organizational Change and Skills Transformation thus serves the role of the connective tissue that collaborates people, processes, technology, and culture in enterprises that are AI-enabled.

4.5.1 The Strategic Imperative for Human-Centered AI Transformation

AI brings an overhaul in the operating models of organizations. Authority to make decisions gradually becomes data-enhanced, workflows are partially or entirely automated, and workers are supposed to work together with intelligent systems. Such changes break the traditional norms and demand deliberate changes of direction.

Organizational Change Management furnishes the rigorous structure needed to drive this move. It integrates the stakeholder analysis, communication plan, leadership alignment, capability building, and behavioral reinforcement in a fairly coherent action program. Notably, OCM does not view AI as a threat to the workforce but as a facilitator of higher value human contribution.

Meanwhile, skills transformation provides that employees have competencies, needed to work in AI-augmented settings. This does not only involve technical literacy but also critical thinking, interpreting data, ethical judgment and adaptive learning skills. Companies that view AI adoption as a technology implementation without making similar investments in people preparedness normally achieve a small part of the projected value.

4.5.2 Ensuring Successful Adoption of AI Solutions

One of the common trends in digital transformation is that, technology failures tend to be disguised failures to adopt. AI solutions can be effective during testing but fail to bring a business impact when the employees do not trust in them, do not understand them, or cannot use them consistently.

The Organizational Change Management creates the channel to long term uptake. Good programs will start with intensive stakeholder mapping to establish those who will be affected, influence groups, and possible areas of resistance. Ready tests assist companies to know the existing attitudes, skills gaps and any cultural obstacles in place prior to the commencement of the deployment.

Communication is a determining factor. The employees need to be certain about:

- why the AI initiative is being implemented,
- how it will affect their roles,
- what support will be provided, and
- what opportunities it creates for career growth.

Training alone is insufficient. Organizations that are performing at a high-level complement formal training with practical pilots, in-built performance support, peer champions, and feedback loops where users can influence the solution. The adoption of AI tools grows at a very rapid rate when employees feel that they are part of its development and changes.

4.5.3 Integrating Processes, People and Technology

AI often does not work well with existing operating models. It tends to redistribute decision rights, bring in new flows of data, and alter cross-functional dependencies. Devoid of the intentional alignment, organizations are likely to produce intelligent tools that will work within the organizational silos.

The role of the professionals of the Organizational Change Management is orchestration critical. They support the process redesign workshops mapping of the current workflows, localizing areas of friction, and the definition of the future-state operating models. New positions should be defined, including AI product owners, model risk managers, data stewards, and automation supervisors, and put in place as part of governance structures.

Leadership alignment is as well an important aspect. Top managers should show a single perspective of the strategic intent of AI. This is because mixed messages of the leadership are some of the quickest means of sabotaging the transformation efforts. Formalized governance and decision-making structures, and responsibility lines can be used to make sure that AI projects are integrated into the corporate fabric, but not run as isolated projects.

4.5.4 Establishing Trust in AI by Transparency.

The currency of AI adoption is trust. There are numerous AI systems most of which are opaque to end users especially when they rely on complex machine learning models. Since there is no way that employees can tell how a system arrives at the conclusions it makes, some level of skepticism is bound to arise.

This challenge can be tackled by Organizational Change Management by employing conscious transparency strategies. These include:

- plain-language explanations of AI capabilities and limitations,
- model interpretability dashboards where appropriate,
- open forums for employee questions and concerns,
- involvement of end users in use-case design, and
- clear articulation of human oversight mechanisms.

Trust building is especially critical in high-stakes sectors such as healthcare, financial services, education, and the public sector. Perceived opacity in such settings can easily become resistance to operations or reputational risk.

The effective demystification of AI by organisations usually positions it clearly and distinctly as a decision support tool, but not a decision replacement. Such framing still maintains human control but showcases the effects of intelligent systems augmentation

4.5.5 Reducing Fear and Workforce Resistance

The issue of job replacement is one of the most emotional in terms of AI adoption. Although the leadership conveys the message that AI is meant to complement, but not to substitute the human workers, it may lead to anxiety and passive resistance due to the uncertainty on the role relevance in future.

These concerns are met by effective Organizational Change Management. Instead of general assurances, the front runners offer actual channels of evolution of workforce. These typically include:

- role impact assessments that clarify which tasks—not jobs—are being automated,
- reskilling and upskilling programs tied to emerging roles,
- internal mobility pathways,
- phased implementation timelines, and
- personalized coaching for highly impacted groups.

The tone of communication matters greatly. Leadership should have compassionate and transparent messages which create credibility. Once the employees realise that their future employability is being actively invested in, resistance often turns into defensive involvement and ultimately becomes promotion.

4.5.6 Accelerating the Realization of AI Value

The implementation of an AI solution is just the first stage of the value cycle. The actual ROI comes about upon the incorporation of new behaviors in day-to-day operations. The Organizational Change Management means that the post-implementation phase will have the same level of attention as the initial rollout.

Normally sustained reinforcement mechanisms will entail:

- usage analytics and adoption dashboards,
- performance metrics tied to AI-enabled workflows,
- continuous learning modules,
- user communities of practice,
- periodic health checks, and
- structured feedback channels to refine models and processes.

OCM teams also monitor "change saturation"—the cumulative burden of concurrent initiatives on the workforce. AI programs that do not consider capacity within the organization tend to experience change fatigue, which may quietly sacrifice adoption.

Well-done reinforcement would transform AI into an acceptance of a new tool, which becomes an unnoticed and trusted part of daily decision-making.

4.5.7 Enabling Agile and Iterative Transformation

The AI applications are hardly deployed in a linear, single deployment model as has been the case with traditional enterprise systems. They are developed in the form of pilots, proofs of concepts, retraining of models, and cycle of improvement. Such iterative character necessitates a similar change in the management of change.

Agile delivery principles are becoming more and more consistent with the modern OCM practices. Organizations move towards incremental releases with the help of constant interaction rather than big, rare change waves. The change managers are involved in the sprint review, retrospective, and prioritization of the backlog to make sure that the human aspect is change-evolving with the technology.

This strategy would create a test-and-learn culture throughout the business. Employees are habituated to gradual improvement as compared to the disruptive and high scale change events. In the long-term, this creates resilience and flexibility within the organization-qualities which become crucial to AI-driven settings.

4.5.8 Strengthening Organizational Culture in the Age of AI

The use of AI eventually puts down to the ground the cultural norms. There are numerous organizations that have to change:

- Away to data-based decision-making through intuition,
- From hierarchical control to cross-functional collaboration,
- From risk avoidance to disciplined experimentation, and
- From static roles to continuous skill evolution.

Organizational Change Management plays a central role in guiding this cultural shift. Culture change cannot be achieved through messaging only, it must be supported with consistent leader actions, revised performance rewards, new talent practices, and visible success stories, which offer support of new ways of working.

This is especially the case with leadership modeling. The senior executives literally using AI-generated insights in how they make decisions is a strong signal to the organization. On the same note, desired behaviors are institutionalized through recognition programs that are reward based on data-driven innovation.

In the long run, the culture of curiosity, evidence-based thinking, and comfort with human-machine cooperation becomes established in the successful integrating organizations that adopt AI.

4.5.9 Enabling Governance, Ethics, and Accountable AI.

With the growth of AI usage, the issues of bias, privacy, explainability, and accountability become even more ethical. The creation of responsible AI cannot be left to the technical teams only but it has to be involved at the company level.

Organizational Change Management works by instilling ethical consciousness on the daily operations. This includes:

- Cross-functional governance forums,
- Clear model accountability structures,
- Bias monitoring protocols,
- Employee education on responsible AI principles, and
- Stakeholder engagement beyond the organization, where appropriate.

OCM professionals often act as translators between technical teams, legal functions, risk management, HR, and business leaders. Their presence will make sure that ethical protection is no longer viewed as a compliance box but rather a component of the design.

Companies that act in advance in matters related to ethics are likely to enjoy a better stakeholder trust and will not suffer expensive reputation losses.

Skills Re-skilling of the AI-powered Workforce.

In line with change management, building of workforce capabilities should scale. The age of AI requires a stratified skills approach that is organizational-wide.

On the fundamental level, there should be AI literacy in the broadest sense so that employees grasp what AI can and cannot accomplish. At the practitioner level, the more expert abilities, like those in data science, machine learning engineering, prompt engineering, and model governance, should be created or learned. At the top management grade, the executives must be fluent enough to make informed strategic decisions regarding AI investments and risks.

A high-maturity organization normally follows the portfolio approach that encompasses:

- Enterprise-wide digital and data literacy programs,
- Role-based technical academies,
- Partnerships with academic institutions,
- Internal talent marketplaces,

- Experiential learning through pilot projects, and
- Continuous learning ecosystems supported by AI-driven learning platforms.

Equally important are durable human skills—critical thinking, ethical reasoning, creativity, collaboration, and adaptive learning—which become more valuable as routine tasks are automated.

In the enterprises that are AI based, the technological sophistication is required, yet the sufficient condition is insufficient. The sustainable value is achieved only when the human transition and technical deployment are coordinated successfully by the organizations. The formal discipline needed to attain this balance is brought by Organizational Change Management and Skills Transformation.

The organizations can take the step of new AI adoption, trust, capacity building, cultural congruence, and ethical governance in order to take the step beyond the isolated AI experiments into the enterprise-wide change. Companies that invest in human-oriented change capabilities are always ahead of others who view AI more as a technological update.

With intelligent systems redefining the very nature of work, those organizations who will succeed will be the ones that come to understand a core reality, the future of AI will always be the future of human ability.

4.6 PARTNER AND ECOSYSTEM COLLABORATION

The digital economy enables companies to generate value through their cooperative relationships with other organizations. Organizations depend on their capacity to establish partnerships with external businesses for better market access and additional product options and faster innovation speed. The interconnected system known as a partner ecosystem has emerged as a basic component that businesses use to drive their operational changes and update their platform systems (Grimm, 2025).

Organizations now expect complete solutions that connect multiple systems because they are moving to cloud-based systems and data platforms and AI-powered services. Organizations need to unite their technology providers and system integrators and independent software vendors and distributors and strategic alliance partners to meet their customer expectations. Organizations now use partner and ecosystem collaboration as a fundamental business process because it enables them to grow their operations and build their capacity for future business growth. Organizations that build their ecosystems through planned design and governance and active implementation will achieve better innovation results and market entry success and distinct customer experience delivery.

4.6.1 Understanding the Partner Ecosystem

A partner ecosystem is an organization over which several organizations cooperate with one another to market, sell, build, deliver or support complementary products and services with the same customer segments. In contrast to the conventional bilateral relationships, the ecosystems are multi-party networks where value is co-created by the coordinated interactions.

Effective ecosystems are defined by three basic principles:

- Mutually creating value in which every participant brings special capabilities.
- Network amplification in which the reach of the networks is larger than that of individuals.
- Customer-based integration in which products are integrated in order to address multifaceted requirements.

The main role of the ecosystem orchestrator, who is usually the platform owner, in this model is to facilitate interoperability, incentive compatibility, and ecosystem health. Partners do not necessarily engage directly, but they are in touch with each other on the same platforms, governance modes, and go-to-market moves.

4.6.2 Strategic Importance of Ecosystem Collaboration

The emergence of ecosystem-based competition is being propelled forward through various fundamental changes. To begin with, there is the change in customer purchasing behavior. Enterprise buyers are increasingly utilizing referred advisors, integrators and domain experts in the process of solution evaluation. The process of purchasing decisions now involves multiple parties who share responsibility for their execution.

The second digital solution category has grown more complicated than ever before. The current market includes products that integrate cloud infrastructure with analytics and artificial intelligence and cybersecurity systems and specialized industry capabilities. The majority of organizations lack the ability to implement all necessary components as separate entities.

Platform economics create advantages for companies that grow their network connections. Companies that establish active ecosystems experience quicker product development processes and access wider markets while keeping their existing customers.

The main reason for ecosystem collaboration becoming essential to digital transformation execution across various industries.

4.6.3 Business Benefits of a Strong Partner Ecosystem

A powerful partner ecosystem can help organizations expand their potential, faster development, and provide more customer value. Ecosystems are effectively designed and managed can be very powerful sources of innovation, market growth, and operational efficiency.

- Gains access to more customers using the existing relationship with customers and the regional presence of partners.
- Reduces the length of the sales cycle and quality of leads based on partner-driven opportunities.
- Facilitates faster innovation through the sharing of similar resources, talents, and expertise.
- It eliminates redundancy of work through the integration of complementary capabilities.
- Enables quicker reaction to the dynamic market demands due to collectively developed products.

- Enhances the value of solutions through the bundling of products and services into integrated services.
- Develops more sources of revenue through cross-selling and upselling.
- Enhances end-to-end, multi-partition customer experience.
- Dilutes business risk in the exploration of new markets or embracing new technologies.
- Grows deal sizes and successful win bids as a result of more holistic, powerful value propositions.
- Reduces customer acquisition expenses by having joint marketing and integrated go-to-market activities.
- Allows typical expansive growth without corresponding additions to internal staff.
- Expands sales, implementation, and support services out of the core organization.
- Increases market credibility through a strong system of partners.
- Enhances retention of customers with integrated, full-stack solution delivery.

4.6.4 Typology of Ecosystem Partners

A mature partner ecosystem typically includes multiple categories of partners, each contributing distinct value.

- **Technology partners** provide complementary platforms or components that integrate with the core offering, often through APIs and interoperability standards.
- **Independent Software Vendors (ISVs)** create specific applications that add the platform functionality, especially in industry-specific cases.
- **Alliance partners** are profound strategic partnerships including co-development, co-marketing and joint solution roadmap.

- **Resellers and Value-Added Resellers (VARs)** are interested in distribution and customer acquisition and they add value to what they offer by customization and support services.
- **Distributors** scale reach by managing logistics, inventory, and reseller enablement.
- **System Integrators (SIs) and Global System Integrators (GSIs)** play a critical role in business settings through the design and execution of multifaceted transformation initiatives and the impacting of significant buying choices.
- Ecosystems with high performance have a specific intention of developing a balanced combination of types of partners in order to have the most coverage of the value chain.

4.6.5 Building an Effective Partner Ecosystem

In order to create an ecosystem with high impact one must be disciplined.

1. **Finding the Right Partners:** The initial action that any organization needs to take is to come up with an ideal partner profile in accordance with the strategic goals. The key performance indicators include complimentary offerings, shared target customers, technical and commercial capability, and compatibility on culture. Strict market analysis prevents unnecessary or out-of-line alliances.
2. **Hiring and Retaining Partners:** Creative recruitment is reliant on a strong partner value proposition. Future partners need to understand the mutual advantages of the business, platform differentiation, model of collaboration and potential of growth in the long term very clearly. Long-term relationships require alignment with executives and clear expectations.
3. **Onboarding and enablement of Partners:** Extensive onboarding has a substantial impact on productivity in the ecosystem. Top programs offer formal training, certification programs, technical documentation, co-marketing resources, portals, and incentive systems. Enabling partners will have

a much higher chance of creating a pipeline and producing consistent customer delivery.

4. **Creating Partnership Go-to-Market Motions:** The clearly defined collaboration models that are required in revenue realization include co-building, co-selling, co-marketing, co-innovation, and co-delivery. To maintain momentum, regular account mapping and joint planning sessions are suitable to keep all teams on track.
5. **Activating the Ecosystem:** Mature ecosystems do not emphasize the creation of value at the individual partnership level, but at the network level. Organizations are to promote cross-partner engagement and organize community discussions and partner meetings, and constantly improve programs based on performance data.

4.6.6 Common Challenges in Ecosystem Collaboration

Ecosystem development brings in a number of challenges that have kept reoccurring regardless of its merits.

- The adoption of digital transformation in the healthcare industry and other associated fields is quickly redefining the process of service delivery within the organizations, data management, and relationships with the users.
- Conditional upon the presence of robust infrastructure, effective regulatory adherence, and the incorporation of new technologies like digital platforms and automation, success cannot be achieved without them.
- The key aspects in respect of ensuring the digital initiatives create real value are user-centered design, workforce preparedness and continuous quality improvement.
- Companies must align on the issue of innovation and risk management, information security and privacy concerns.
- The common electronic platforms and interoperability systems improve coordination, scale and efficiency of stakeholders.

- The digital era of business is more about collaborative models, including B2B2C models and ecosystems.
- Even with the strengths, challenges that are to be addressed properly are legacy system, skills gap, resistance to change, and governance complexities.
- Generalizing the findings, long-term leadership dedication, plan, and constant surveillance are critical to the success of digital transformation efforts in the long term.

4.6.7 Role of Technology in Ecosystem Enablement

Digital platforms are necessary for expanding ecosystem collaboration through their ability to support partnership growth. The current Partner Relationship Management (PRM) systems work together with Customer Relationship Management (CRM) software to create an integrated view of sales opportunities and client accounts and partner achievements. The system offers essential features which include partner portals and deal registration and co-selling workflow support and marketing automation integration and analytics dashboards and secure data sharing. The tools help organizations to decrease channel conflicts while they establish better operational ties and create improved experiences for their business partners. Co-selling platforms become essential tools for enterprise environments because these organizations need to manage multiple partner relationships which will lead to shared customer connections. Structured orchestration improves efficiency and increases win probability.

4.6.8 Metrics and Measurement of Ecosystem Performance

The maintenance of ecosystem value entails efficient systems of measurement. Data-driven understanding helps the organizations to determine the best performing partners as they formulate their practices of collaboration. The traditional indicators applied to assess the ecosystem health are partner sourced and partner influenced pipeline, revenue contribution by partner type, engagement and activation rates, joint win rates, customer retention and time-to-revenue of new partners. At high-level organizations assess the success of their partners along the customer lifecycle and develop formal ecosystem playbooks defining operational roles and best practices in engaging with partners.

4.6.9 The Future of Partner Ecosystems

Organizations will need to establish partner ecosystems because digital platforms will continue to develop more effectively through their ecosystem relationships. Organizations now use data analytics and artificial intelligence to create better systems that help them find suitable partners and enhance their operational efficiency. Companies now establish industry-specific ecosystems because businesses require particular vertical knowledge that extends beyond general expertise. Organizations need to adopt open standards because multi-cloud and multi-platform systems create higher demands for system compatibility through their open system requirements. The three elements of trust, governance and ethical data sharing procedures have become essential requirements for successful business outcomes. Organizations that invest early in ecosystem maturity will be better positioned to compete in platform-dominated markets.

Partner and ecosystem collaboration has become a cornerstone capability for modern digital enterprises. Organizations that create network partners with complementary strengths to their business will achieve higher market presence through enhanced innovation processes and unified customer service delivery. Ecosystem success needs organizations to select their partners through intentional methods which include building support systems and executing their marketing strategies with proper technological backing and ongoing performance assessment. Organizations that develop successful governance systems for their business ecosystems will enjoy increased growth potential through digital economy changes.

4.7 SUMMARY

The chapter showed how organizations implement digital transformation through their operational processes while demonstrating that all governance elements and operational workflows and technological methods and staff and business alliances must work together to achieve enduring success. The study proved that successful transformation requires organizations to apply contemporary technologies while building effective governance structures and risk control systems and adopting Agile and DevOps work methods and updating their operational procedures for better performance and customer service. The elements enable organizations to transform their business operations through integrated digital solutions which reach all parts of their organization.

The chapter presented the transformation of human aspects and ecosystem components as two essential elements for operational success. The organization needed to establish readiness through proper change management and continuous skills development because these factors would help them achieve better adoption results and decrease resistance. Organizations needed to establish strong partner relationships and ecosystem networks because these connections would help them gain new capabilities and speed up their innovation processes while delivering value at a larger scale. The chapter revealed that organizations require a cohesive strategy that incorporates a structured implementation system with cultural matching and cooperative growth plans to establish a digital revolution that prepares their business to the new challenges in the future.

Multiple Choice Questions (MCQs)

1. **What is the primary objective of transformation execution in digital initiatives?**

   A. Increase hardware capacity

   B. Align strategy with implementation and deliver business value

   C. Reduce employee headcount

   D. Eliminate legacy systems completely

2. **Which of the following is a key component of effective governance in transformation programs?**

   A. Ignoring stakeholder feedback

   B. Centralized decision-making without accountability

   C. Clear roles, responsibilities, and decision rights

   D. Avoiding performance metrics

3. **Risk management in transformation initiatives primarily focuses on:**

   A. Eliminating all risks

   B. Identifying, assessing, and mitigating risks

   C. Transferring all risks to vendors

   D. Ignoring low-probability risks

4. **What is a core principle of Agile methodology?**

   A. Fixed scope and rigid planning

   B. Sequential development phases

   C. Iterative development and continuous feedback

   D. Delayed customer involvement

5. **DevOps primarily aims to:**

   A. Separate development and operations teams

   B. Increase manual processes

   C. Improve collaboration and automate delivery pipelines

   D. Replace Agile practices

6. **Business process modernization involves:**

   A. Preserving outdated workflows

   B. Digitizing and optimizing business processes

   C. Eliminating all manual intervention

   D. Focusing only on IT systems

7. **Organizational change management is essential because it:**
   A. Focuses only on technology upgrades
   B. Ensures employees adopt and sustain new ways of working
   C. Reduces the need for leadership involvement
   D. Avoids training requirements

8. **Skills transformation in digital initiatives requires:**
   A. Hiring only external consultants
   B. Ignoring existing workforce capabilities
   C. Continuous learning, reskilling, and upskilling
   D. Eliminating legacy skills completely

9. **Partner and ecosystem collaboration helps organizations by:**
   A. Increasing dependency without benefits
   B. Limiting innovation
   C. Leveraging external expertise and accelerating transformation
   D. Reducing scalability

10. **Which of the following best summarizes successful transformation execution?**
   A. Technology-first approach without people considerations
   B. One-time implementation with no iteration
   C. Integrated approach combining governance, agility, people, and partnerships
   D. Complete outsourcing of all processes

Answers

1	2	3	4	5	6	7	8	9	10
B	C	B	C	C	B	B	C	C	C

Chapter 5
Value Measurement and Future Enterprise Platforms

5.1 OVERVIEW

The implementation is no longer the priority as organizations proceed on the digital transformation paths; instead, the priority is on the quantifiable value generation and performance growth. Technology projects are no longer evaluated based on achievement of delivery but on how it can contribute to strategic performance outcome of growth of revenues, efficiency, customer satisfaction, and resilience of the organization. The chapter reviews how businesses can develop disciplined ways of measuring business value and ROI to ensure that digital investments are not only oriented to overall business strategies but also have well-developed performance measurement systems.

Simultaneously, the major organizations understand that change is a sustained process and not a program. Modern KPI systems, continuous improvement models, and technology strategy that looks into the future will help organizations to adapt to the rapidly changing environments and stay competitive. This chapter discusses consequently the measures, best practices, and emerging technology trends in the enterprise that together will enable the formation of a future-ready Digital Enterprise, who is data-driven, agile, and poised to achieve sustainable growth and development in the long term.

5.2 BUSINESS VALUE AND ROI ASSESSMENT

A Business Value Assessment (BVA) is a structured, data-driven methodology used to quantify the potential and realized value of a proposed solution, strategic initiative, or technology investment. Its primary purpose is to establish a clear and defensible linkage between organizational investments and measurable business outcomes. Organizations in the present time need to demonstrate their financial advantages through business value assessments because people now review their digital expenditures with greater scrutiny than before (Finesse, 2025).

The BVA method needs proper implementation because it gives complete results about a project's value to an organization. The system assesses direct financial outcomes together with its impact on operational success and consumer satisfaction and risk management and employee efficiency and business growth. The initiative shows its value to decision-makers through its complete assessment of enterprise value development.

5.2.1 Strategic Role of Business Value Assessment

Business Value Assessment functions as an essential element for contemporary business operations which require digital transformation through cloud migration and artificial intelligence implementation and platform modernization. Organizations today face challenges which require solutions that extend beyond their existing intuitive decision-making methods. Executives need structured proof which shows that their proposed projects will generate substantial returns on investment.

A strong BVA system enables leadership teams to choose investment projects according to their future value projections while it brings different stakeholders together through common goals and it helps them make precise capital distribution decisions. The system assists organizations in portfolio rationalization by showing which projects will create the most significant strategic and financial advantages. BVA functions as both a pre-investment validation instrument and a post-implementation value tracking system which enables organizations to monitor their actual gains against anticipated outcomes.

5.2.2 Current-State Assessment

The BVA process starts with an organization-wide assessment that evaluates its present condition. This phase establishes the baseline against which future improvements will be measured. The study examines all operational workflows together with their technological environment and cost structures and performance indicators and existing challenges.

The research uses quantitative data which includes cycle times and error rates and infrastructure costs and revenue leakage, and it uses qualitative data which stakeholders provided through their interview and workshop participation and process observation. The dual lens approach helps to identify both apparent operational inefficiencies and hidden organizational conflicts. The current-state assessment process establishes an accurate operational base, which prevents organizations from making excessive optimistic predictions about their future performance. The business case demonstrates operational challenges through its current-state assessment, which establishes a factual basis for the proposal.

The current stage of work discovers previously unidentified value streams. The organization has multiple areas for development through its existing processes which include manual work duplication and its current data systems and unused resources. The assessment process becomes more trustworthy when we identify their crucial areas at an earlier stage.

5.2.3 Future-State Vision and Value Drivers

The BVA establishes a measurable future-state vision after completing its baseline assessment. The vision defines success criteria which will be measured after the proposed initiative achieves implementation. The system normally delivers enhancements which include faster operations, reduced costs, improved quality, better scalability, higher customer satisfaction, and enhanced risk management capabilities.

The process requires organizations to identify their value drivers which function as specific methods their benefits will be achieved through. The following value drivers represent the standard elements which drive value creation:

- Revenue growth through enhanced customer acquisition or retention
- Cost reduction via automation or infrastructure optimization
- Productivity gains from workflow simplification
- Risk mitigation through improved controls and compliance
- Working capital improvements through faster cycle times

Explicitly mapping initiatives to value drivers ensures traceability between proposed actions and expected outcomes. It also makes financial modelling more reliable and increases the executive trust in the potential gains.

5.2.4 Quantifying Tangible and Intangible Value

The BVA system demonstrates its effectiveness through its capacity to assess both measurable and non-measurable advantages. Tangible value typically includes measurable financial improvements such as cost savings, revenue uplift, margin expansion, and headcount efficiency. These elements form the backbone of traditional ROI calculations.

Digital enterprises now recognize that intangible value has grown into a critical asset for their operations. Improvements in employee experience, customer trust, brand perception, decision quality, and organizational agility may not immediately translate into direct financial gains but often have significant long-term impact. Mature BVAs incorporate proxy metrics, benchmarking data, and structured estimation techniques to assign defensible value ranges to these softer benefits.

The process of assessing transformation initiatives requires organizations to establish an equilibrium point between their measurable and unmeasurable benefits because organizations need to evaluate transformational changes which provide strategic advantages beyond their immediate financial worth.

5.2.5 Financial Modeling: ROI, TCO, and Payback

Business Value Assessment relies on financial rigor as its fundamental requirement. The financial models use quantified benefits and estimated costs as their core elements to perform objective investment option evaluations. The most common key metrics include the following measurements:

- **Return on Investment (ROI):** Measures the net financial gain relative to investment cost.
- **Total Cost of Ownership (TCO):** Captures full lifecycle costs, including implementation, operation, maintenance, and decommissioning.
- **Payback Period:** Indicates how quickly the investment recovers its initial cost.
- **Net Present Value (NPV):** The method discounts upcoming cash payments to calculate their worth in present time which reflects the monetary value of time.
- **Internal Rate of Return (IRR):** The method delivers a standardized measurement which shows the anticipated returns of an investment.

The system uses multiple performance scenarios together with their sensitivity ranges and all potential risk factors to create a complete model which real-life situations. The method increases trustworthiness with financial experts and investment decision-making groups.

5.2.6 Stakeholder Alignment and Decision Support

Beyond financial analysis, BVAs serve as powerful tools for stakeholder alignment. Large-scale initiatives require organizations to balance conflicting priorities which exist between their business units and technology teams and finance and operations functions. The implementation of transparent evidence-based assessments establishes a common reference point which decreases operational hurdles and speeds up the process of making decisions.

The collaboration of Effective BVAs with multiple stakeholders allows them to gather input from executive sponsors, process owners, IT architects, finance analysts, and end users. The inclusive method of this research increases both assumption accuracy and the probability of adoption in future processes. The analysis results in higher organizational acceptance when stakeholders observe their viewpoints being represented.

A well-organized BVA structure delivers executives specific decision-making paths which allow them to choose between continuing, postponing, expanding, or redesigning an initiative.

5.2.7 Communicating the Business Case

The way that assessment results are shared with others determines their effect on business value assessments. The results of a complete study will not change any decision when the study results are shown through complex technical language. The BVA results at high-performing organizations function as executive summaries which receive backing from numerical data.

Effective communication typically includes: →

- Clearly articulated assumptions
- Transparent methodology
- Visual representations of value pools
- Scenario comparisons
- Risk considerations
- Implementation roadmap

The objective is to make the value story intuitive, credible, and actionable. The executive audience needs to understand quickly the likely payoff, the weight given to it, and the critical argument's support.

5.2.8 Value Realization and Continuous Validation

A common weakness in many organizations is treating the BVA as a one-time pre-investment exercise. The approach reaches its highest worth when organizations use it as a continuous value evaluation method. The post-implementation tracking process assesses actual performance by comparing it to expected benefits which allows necessary adjustments to be made.

Continuous validation serves several purposes. The process tracks service delivery results to establish responsibility for results while it detects user adoption issues at an early stage and uses concrete evidence to improve future business case development. Organizations that establish value realization as their standard operating procedure will achieve better forecasting performance and improved investment oversight capabilities over time.

Digital environments that experience rapid changes need companies to conduct regular assessments because market conditions and user behavior and technological capabilities can transform without warning.

5.2.9 Best Practices for High-Quality Business Value Assessments

Organizations must use a number of best practices to optimize when undertaking BVAs. To start with, goals should be clearly stated and geared towards enterprise strategy. The study shows that when organizations establish their objectives without clear direction their analysis work becomes unfocused and their results become less valid.

The data collection process must include multiple data collection methods. Financial data should not be treated as the only essential information because organizations need to understand operational data and experiential value drivers. The assessment process becomes more effective when organizations combine system data with process metrics and stakeholder input and external benchmarks.

The process needs analytical rigor as its third requirement. The team must document their assumptions while performing sensitivity analysis and they should establish standardized methods whenever possible. The field increases both repeatability and auditability.

The communication should target executive decision-makers instead of only technical audiences. The organization will use BVAs as part of its continuous improvement process which requires periodic assessments to confirm that projected value has been achieved.

Business Value Assessment has become a vital skill of contemporary online companies. Companies need to use complete evidence-based valuation methods because their technology investments have grown in size and complexity beyond what single financial metrics and intuition can measure. An effective BVA does not only enhance investment decisions, it also creates cross-functional alignment, enhances accountability, and speeds up realization of values.

The complete set of Business Value Assessment enables organizations to link their strategic goals with financial resources and technology systems and operational capabilities. Organizations that implement this discipline within their operations gain improved investment confidence and operational effectiveness and achieve maximum economic and strategic results from their transformation initiatives.

5.3 CONTINUOUS IMPROVEMENT MODELS

Organizations need to adopt continuous improvement as their main operational method for maintaining competitive advantages in industries that experience rapid market changes. Continuous improvement defines a dedicated process which organization use to develop their products and services and operational systems and staff capabilities through both small upgrades and major technological changes. The practice of continuous improvement has expanded beyond quality control departments and now operates throughout all business functions which include product development and customer service and operational systems and partnership networks (Rehkopf, 2025).

The speed at which businesses transform their operations through digital technology requires them to establish permanent mechanisms for organizational enhancement. Organizations must implement continuous performance monitoring to address multiple requirements that arise from their need to execute rapid software releases and make decisions based on data and their platform-based operational frameworks. The continuous improvement models establish essential governance structures and essential discipline systems and essential feedback routes which enable organizations to convert their operational knowledge into measurable economic success. The complete implementation of these systems establishes an environment which promotes knowledge acquisition and organizational flexibility while supporting evidence-based processes that help organizations achieve sustained value creation.

5.3.1 Conceptual Foundations of Continuous Improvement

Continuous improvement is anchored on the notion that the performance of an organization can be continuously improved by systematic study and disciplined action. Instead of adopting the ad hoc approach to change through the occasional transtformation efforts, continuous improvement encourages the continuous cycle of assessment, testing and improvement. This thinking is similar to the agile, responsive, and customer-focused concepts of the current digital operating models.

Generally, there are two general modes of improvement. Incremental improvement aims at small and frequent improvements which compound in the long run to make great improvements in efficiency and quality. In comparison, breakthrough improvement is more radical redesign or innovation which brings step change performance benefits. Successful enterprises will follow both strategies in a balanced portfolio, with incremental techniques used to stabilize and optimize the major business operations, and breakthrough initiatives set aside as the means of strategic change.

Notably, continuous improvement is not a pure technical process. It is largely reliant on the leadership dedication, cross-functional teamwork, clear measurement, and the culture promoting experimentation without the fear of failure. Most organizations that consider improvement as a one-time venture, instead of a continuous ability, fail to maintain transformation results.

5.3.2 The Plan–Do–Check–Act (PDCA) Cycle

One of the best-used continuous improvement models is the Plan-Do-Check-Act (PDCA) cycle, which is a four-step model of the iterative process based on experimental learning with discipline. The PDCA cycle offers a systematic approach of experimenting changes, confirming findings and generalizing successful changes on a larger scale throughout the enterprise.

Plan: It starts with the identification of an opportunity to make improvements according to performance data, customer feedback, or strategic priorities. The stage includes problem definition, root causes analysis, and defining success metrics and designing a proposed intervention. The key characteristics of good planning include good speculation and articulation to business goals.

Do: The proposed change is introduced in a controlled or pilot phase during the execution phase. Minimal scope helps to minimize risk and allows quick learning. This step can be used in digital settings, where automation, feature flags, or sandbox environments are used to safely test changes.

Check: During the evaluation stage, both quantitative and qualitative data are used to determine whether the change achieved the intended results. They have teams that measure actual results against baseline measures and predetermined success measures. This step reinforces the fact-driven aspect of contemporary constant improvement.

Act: In case the change is successful then it is standardized and scaled down to wider operations. In case of unsatisfactory results, better understanding is garnered and the process starts all over again with new modified hypotheses. Organizations adopt iterative PDCA cycles as their standard method which leads to continuous performance enhancements. The PDCA method enables digital mature companies to use automated systems for monitoring and telemetry and analytics platforms which deliver faster feedback than traditional quality control methods.

5.3.3 Major Continuous Improvement Methodologies

While PDCA provides the foundational cycle, several complementary methodologies exist to implement continuous improvement across large-scale operations. The system provides different tools together with multiple viewpoints which organizations use to create their own customized solution.

1. **Lean Management:** Lean concentrates on delivering maximum customer value through its waste reduction efforts. The process requires organizations to optimize their activities by removing all elements that do not contribute to value creation. The implementation of Lean principles in digital environments supports value stream mapping and workflow optimization and cycle time reduction efforts.
2. **Six Sigma:** Six Sigma uses statistical methods to achieve its goals of decreasing process variation and defect rates. The structured framework of DMAIC (Define Measure Analyze Improve Control) enables organizations running Six Sigma operations to achieve success in high-reliability environments which demand precise results. Six Sigma now uses advanced analytics and machine learning to improve its diagnostic capabilities.
3. **Total Quality Management (TQM):** TQM establishes complete organizational responsibility for quality control which requires organizations to focus on customers and engage their employees while conducting ongoing performance assessments. The program established fundamental cultural principles which modern improvement methods still use to create companywide quality control standards.
4. **DevOps and Agile Feedback Loops:** Agile and DevOps practices serve as modern approaches to continuous improvement in software-intensive enterprises. The combination of continuous integration with continuous delivery and automated testing alongside observability tools creates rapid feedback systems which duplicate traditional improvement processes while speeding up their execution.

Organizations now adopt hybrid models which combine Lean efficiency with Six Sigma standards and Agile flexibility and DevOps automation to create a unified system for process improvement.

5.3.4 Continuous vs. Continual Improvement

Continuous and continual improvement processes remain distinct from each other according to some practitioners who use these terms as synonyms. Organizations use continuous improvement to refer to their ongoing process of making small improvements to current operations which they manage through statistical process control and operational optimization methods. The term continual improvement functions as a broader concept which includes both incremental changes and major transformational developments.

The practical needs of an enterprise require better operational systems than the actual distinction between two things which needs resolution. Organizations that have reached advanced development stages implement three distinct improvement processes which include real-time optimization, tactical process redesign, and enterprise-wide strategic innovation. The system provides an extensive improvement framework which enables organizations to handle both small operational problems and major organizational changes.

5.3.5 Embedding Continuous Improvement in Digital Operating Models

The organization needs to integrate continuous improvement into its operating model because it requires permanent value delivery. Digital enterprises achieve this integration through several reinforcing mechanisms.

Organizations need to install comprehensive process tracking systems which provide instant access to their process performance metrics. The second step requires organizations to form cross-departmental teams which take responsibility for complete product results instead of only their specific functions. The third step involves organizations using CI/CD pipelines and observability platforms together with AI-based analytics to create automated feedback mechanisms.

Platform-based architectures create enhanced capability to improve systems through their process of establishing standardized services and data models and integration patterns. The established standards of the system reduce system variability which enables easier detection of performance trends and their subsequent optimization. The cloud-native environments allow organizations to conduct large-scale experiments which lead to quick improvement cycles for their operations.

Organizations that successfully embed continuous improvement into their digital fabric demonstrate higher release velocity and better service reliability and faster incident recovery and increased customer satisfaction metrics.

5.3.6 Measurement and Data-Driven Optimization

Organizations need accurate data to identify their performance deficiencies and to confirm the success of their interventions and to maintain their progress throughout time. Organizations today dedicate significant resources to develop comprehensive performance assessment systems which integrate their operational data with customer feedback and financial performance metrics.

The primary measurement methods include the following practices.

- Establishing baseline performance metrics before interventions
- Defining leading and lagging indicators
- Implementing real-time dashboards and observability tools
- Applying advanced analytics and AI for pattern detection
- Linking improvement metrics to business value outcomes

Importantly, measurement systems must balance precision with usability. Overly complex metrics frameworks result in reporting exhaustion which decreases essential focus on important tasks. High-performing organizations prioritize a small set of meaningful, outcome-oriented indicators that directly support decision-making and value realization.

5.3.7 Cultural and Leadership Enablers

Sustainable continuous improvement produces an organizational culture which functions as its final result. Leadership plays a crucial role in establishing an atmosphere that supports experimental work while teams learn from their mistakes and gain authority to challenge current processes.

The psychological safety, openness in performance metrics, appreciation of contributions to improvement, and matching incentives to long-term value instead of temporary output can be considered the most important cultural enablers. The participation of the employees is of equal importance; front-line workers usually have some of the most practical information regarding the inefficiencies within the processes.

It is also imperative to have capability development. Companies need to invest in training workers in methods of solving problems, data literacy, process analysis and digital tools. Most of the top businesses have formal academies or centers of excellence where these skills are institutionalized.

5.3.8 From Continuous Improvement to Continuous Innovation

The distinction between continuous improvement and continuous innovation is starting to be erased as digital maturity continues to rise. Companies that learn to optimize incrementally tend to apply the same rigorous learning processes to product innovation, experimentation of a business model, and ecosystem development.

The current pace of evolution has accelerated due to AI technologies and automated systems and advanced analytical methods. It is now possible to predict model opportunities and identify areas of improvement before the decline of performance is noticeable. Autonomous remediation systems can solve particular types of problems without requiring human staff to intervene. The features of these systems have transformed continuous improvement from a response discipline into a proactive intelligence system.

The andragogical approach to continual improvement as it is perceived by future-ready enterprises functions as a strategic driver which enables organizations to achieve operational resilience and adaptability while maintaining their competitive edge.

Continuous improvement models provide organizations with structural frameworks which enable them to optimize their digital performance results. Organizations can develop quantitative business results from their data through the implementation of PDCA Lean Six

Sigma and Agile-DevOps feedback loop frameworks. The combination of these strategies and effective measurement systems creates strong closed-loop learning environments which organizations can use to build digital operating models.

The presence of tools and methods fails to provide sufficient resources for success. Leadership dedication, cultural conformity, interdepartmental cooperation, and sustained capacity building are the keys to success in the long term. To not only position themselves to optimise operations in the current day but also be able to respond in an intelligent way to the disruptions that are bound to happen tomorrow, the organizations that make continuous improvement an institutionalized enterprise capability place themselves in a better position to do so.

5.4 PERFORMANCE METRICS AND KPIS

In the digitally empowered businesses, the value creation is not just about the implementation of the transformation programs but it is also about the measurement of whether the transformation programs deliver valuable results. The needed structure and data-driven basis to monitor progress, assess performance, and a continuous improvement guide is the Performance Metrics and Key performance indicators (KPIs). They serve as the operational nervous system of an enterprise and help its strategic intent to be transformed into quantifiable signals to be used in making decisions at all organizational levels (Geeksforgeeks, 2025c).

The contemporary organizations exist in the setting of high-speed changes in technology, large amounts of data, and increased pressure on stakeholders. In this case, the use of intuition-based management cannot be effective. Leaders need measurable performance in terms of financial, operational, customer and innovation performances. An effective performance measurement framework allows companies to identify an imminent risk, confirm strategic assumptions, make resource allocation efficient, and hold people responsible. As a result, performance metrics and KPIs have taken the center stage of governance of enterprises, digital transformation, and value management (coursera, 2025).

5.4.1 Understanding Performance Metrics

Performance measures- These are quantitative or qualitative measures applied to the efficiency, effectiveness, and wellbeing of business activities, business processes, systems, or individuals. They offer the crude measurement infrastructure whereby organizations track their activities and determine their progress towards the set goals. The metrics differ greatly in industries and functions, but the idea is that the metrics are designed to convert organizational activity into something observable and analyzable.

In the enterprise level, performance metrics play a number of important functions. They help leaders to track the stability of the operational performance, detect the performance gaps, observe the trends, and facilitate the evidence-based decision-making. Another way in which metrics can be used is as an organizational control panel by reviewing them regularly to enable the management decide on whether to maintain, revise, or to do away with certain strategies or initiatives. In digitally mature organizations, metrics are becoming permanently integrated into automated dashboards and real-time observability platforms, and are now able to have almost-instant insights into the state of performance.

Notably, metrics alone are descriptive, meaning that they tell what is occurring. Their strategic strength appears when they are in business-related directions and structured into consistent measurement systems, and this is where KPIs become critical.

5.4.2 Defining Key Performance Indicators (KPIs)

Key Performance Indicators are a narrower category of performance measures, which are clearly linked to strategic goals and key success factors. Although numerous measures can be gathered within the enterprise, KPIs are used to recognize the limited measures that are most significant in assessing the progress of the organization towards the objectives. Simply put, metrics give scope of visibility, and KPIs strategic focus.

Successful KPIs have a number of distinguishing traits. They are quantifiable, time-constrained and business outcome-related. They break down the high-level strategy into actionable targets that can be shaped by teams by their day-to-day work. An organization that operates in digital commerce has the capacity to maintain more than 100 operational metrics but needs to use customer conversion rate and average order value and customer lifetime value as its essential performance indicators which directly support revenue growth.

The KPIs serve to communicate information which creates executive and managerial and frontline team members with shared understanding through their system which transforms complex performance data into a limited set of performance indicators. The system requires implementation in large organizations because their various performance metrics create conflicting business objectives which lead to decreased responsibility.

5.4.3 The Relationship Between Metrics and KPIs

Knowledge of the difference between performance metric and KPIs and their interrelation is critical in developing a powerful measurement architecture. The larger measurement ecosystem is made up of performance metrics, which encompass the detailed information of operations in processes and functions. On the highest level of this hierarchy, KPIs are the most strategically important indicators which are based on the underlying metric base.

A useful way to conceptualize this relationship is through the measurement value chain:

- **Input metrics** measure resources consumed (e.g., hours worked, budget spent).
- **Process metrics** track operational efficiency (e.g., cycle time, throughput).
- **Output metrics** measure immediate results (e.g., features delivered, orders processed).
- **Outcome metrics (KPIs)** evaluate business impact (e.g., revenue growth, customer satisfaction).

Any organization that is more concerned with input or output metrics is likely to fall into the trap of measuring activity but not value. Established businesses gradually move to the focus of the outcome-oriented KPIs that indicate customer impact, financial performance, and strategic progress. This change is especially significant in digital transformation initiatives, where the measures of productivity traditionally used might not reflect innovation value.

5.4.4 Categories of Enterprise KPIs

KPIs are usually working on the multiple organizational levels and each has different decision-making requirements. On the top level, the strategic KPIs give an executive picture of health and long-term improvement in the enterprise. These usually have measures like, return on investment (ROI), revenue growth, market share, and profitability. Due to their high level of scope, senior leadership tends to review strategic KPIs either quarterly or annually.

Operational KPIs aim at a shorter-term performance in business processes or functional areas. These indicators assist the managers to detect any emerging problems and put the corrective measures to make sure that they do not influence the strategic outcomes. These are system uptime, order fulfillment cycle time, and defect rates. Operational KPIs are normally tracked either on a daily or weekly basis and are closely associated with process improvement programs.

Functional KPIs are specific to the departments like marketing, finance, human resource or customer support. These measures give fine-grained information that applies to a focused team and yet is in line with what the enterprise wants to achieve. As an example, the marketing team can monitor the conversion rates of the campaign, and the HR can monitor the employee engagement rating.

The other significant definition means leading and lagging indicators. Primary KPIs are used to give early indicators of future performance (pipeline growth or user engagement) and therefore can be managed actively. Lagging KPIs, in turn, are an indication of the results that will take place (e.g., quarterly revenue). Organizations with good performance have a balance between the two with leading indicators that predict performance and lagging indicators that confirm results.

5.4.5 Functional Performance Metric Domains

In addition to classifying KPI, business organizations usually group performance measures in large functional areas. Financial measures evaluate the health of the economy using the indicators of revenue growth, operating margin, cash flow and total cost of ownership. These metrics are still fundamental since they end up defining the sustainability of an enterprise.

Customer metrics are used to assess the level of effectiveness of the organization in providing value to the customers. Examples are customer satisfaction (CSAT), Net Promoter Score (NPS), retention rate, and customer lifetime value. In online enterprises, customer experience indicators are becoming one of the leading indicators of the revenue achievement.

Operation measures dwell on efficiency and reliability of processes. Cycle time, throughput, defect rates, and service availability are some of the measures that can be used to optimize internal performance and minimize waste. These measures are especially significant in the Devops, manufacturing and service delivery settings.

Employee and workforce measures evaluate the organizational competence and involvement. Productivity, attrition, skill preparedness and training efficacy are some of the indicators, which can give insights on human capital health-a more important aspect in AI-driven enterprises.

Project and innovation measurement monitors the achievement of change projects. These can be time-to-market, feature adoption, the speed of innovation pipeline and success rate of experiments. These metrics become strategic as organizations change their operating models to product-centric ones.

5.4.6 Designing Effective KPIs

Not all KPIs drive value. Badly-constructed indicators may either be confusing, lead to anti-optimal behavior, or overwhelm the decision-maker. The design of KPI, thus, demands that it should have methodological rigor.

One of the most common methods is SMART framework - having KPIs that are Specific, Measurable, Achievable, Relevant and Time bound. Nevertheless, mature businesses go ahead to test the fact of whether every KPI is indeed decision-biased and behavioral. One such test would be the existence of a metric that is obviously actionable. Provided that leaders are not able to decide what decision a KPI should affect, then the indicator may not be strategic.

Congruence is also very important. With KPIs, there should be a logical flow of enterprise strategy to business units, teams, and individuals. This vertical integration guarantees that the optimization of the locals is not compromised by enterprise results. Meanwhile, horizontal alignment among functions makes siloed metrics incompatible with each other.

Lastly, organizations should protect against the growth of metrics. Gathering too many KPIs blurs purpose and extra binding in reports. The prominent businesses tend to have a strict chain of command: a few high-level KPIs are accompanied by gradually lower operation-level indicators.

5.4.7 Data Foundations and Measurement Infrastructure

The quality of data, integration and governance are vital in the process of reliable performance measurement. The presence of inaccurate data and delayed data and disjointed data streams disrupt the effectiveness of optimal KPI framework designs. The modern measurement systems which exist today have become integrated into digital platforms and analytics pipelines and observability tools because organisations now possess advanced digital technology infrastructure.

Information gathering should cover numerous enterprise systems which include ERP systems and CRM systems and HR systems and operational telemetry systems. The process requires data engineering best practices and standardization and metric calculation ownership. Executive confidence is usually lost because organizations that do not align the definition of metrics will end up having multiple versions of the truth.

High-tech businesses are shifting to real-time performance tracking through the implementation of cloud analytics and AI-based insights and automated dashboards. The system enables users to quickly identify abnormal patterns while it performs ongoing value assessments and makes future predictions. The system creates significant problems through its requirement for data governance and privacy protections and ethical data usage practices, particularly in regulated industries.

5.4.8 KPI Governance and Performance Review Cadence

The measurement systems become useful only when organizations implement their use through established governance structures. Organizations that achieve success use formal processes to review their key performance indicators which match the decision-making levels of their operations. The executive dashboards provide monthly or quarterly access to their content while users can monitor operational metrics through daily automated alarm systems.

Governance structures create the foundations for measuring ownership and escalation and remediation processes. The responsible teams need to investigate performance when it falls outside the established targets and they should implement corrective actions. The closed-loop feedback process transforms KPIs into active management tools which function as reports.

The current trend shows that businesses combine their KPI governance requirements with three operational frameworks which include enterprise performance management, DevOps observability and digital value realization offices. The measurement process will establish strong connections with strategic implementation because it will no longer function as an isolated reporting system.

5.4.9 Benefits of a Mature Measurement Framework

When organizations use performance measures and KPIs correctly, they achieve significant organizational benefits. The performance metrics enable organizations to make decisions based on evidence while maintaining their strategic goals and organizational responsibility. The management team will receive quicker access to upcoming hazards and potential benefits which enables them to take proactive measures.

Measurement systems enable organizations to identify process weaknesses which help them to improve their operations through continuous improvement efforts. Customer-centric organizations boost their ability to manage and preserve customer experience through enhanced KPI visibility. The practice of disciplined measurement helps organizations to govern their investments better because it connects technology spending with measurable business outcomes.

The cultural influence holds important value. Open Key Performance Indicators provide mutual understanding of performance and inter-functionality by giving visuals on what success should look like. The cultural alignment becomes the most effective asset which organizations need to transform their digital operations because it enables them to measure their progress.

5.4.10 Limitations and Common Pitfalls

- **Metric overload:** Decision-makers face difficulties in understanding important information because they need to track too many indicators which lack defined priorities.
- **Misalignment with business outcomes:** The organization faces problems because its key performance indicators (KPIs) which focus on specific operational targets lead to local optimization yet decrease overall enterprise value.
- **Gaming the metrics:** The existing incentive program leads teams to produce inaccurate results because its design fails to properly measure actual team performance.
- **Data latency and quality issues:** The outdated systems create data problems because they generate information which arrives later and contains inconsistent and unreliable data that makes measurement results less accurate.
- **Obsolescence of KPIs:** Business models need complete metric reviews because their existing performance measurements need updates to stay relevant.

5.4.11 Toward Intelligent, Value-Driven Measurement

Organizations that have adopted AI and automation and platform-based operating models are now transitioning to performance measurement systems which provide predictive and adaptive measurement capabilities. Future-ready organizations replace their traditional dashboard system with an advanced performance system which uses real-time telemetry and machine learning and scenario modeling.

The new business model requires dynamic linkages between performance indicators and value streams and customer journey paths and product performance metrics. Leading organizations now include experience metrics and ecosystem metrics and sustainability indicators in their measurement portfolios. The expanded perspective shows that enterprise value now exists beyond its previous two-dimensional boundaries.

The management of digital organizations depends on performance indicators together with key performance indicators as their main measurement tools. The organizations need to demonstrate their capacity to generate emotional responses from people and to implement quick and precise decisions according to their historical reporting methods. Companies that view measurement as a tactical asset (not a regulatory practice) will be in the best position to reap long-run value off their investment in transformation.

5.5 EMERGING ENTERPRISE TECHNOLOGY TRENDS

The enterprise technology market is experiencing a revolution that is never been seen before due to the accelerated development of artificial intelligence, hyperconnectivity, automation, and platform-based architectures. Organizations are not merely moving to digital technologies to enhance the efficiency of their operation, instead, they are re-architecting their overall business models to be based on smart, information-driven, and perpetually adaptive platforms. With the increased involvement of companies in the digital business landscape, the convergence of new technologies is changing the value creation, delivery, and measurement processes (Geeksforgeeks, 2025b).

A shift in the nature of digital initiatives, which are presently isolated, to a wholesomely integrated digital ecosystems, is the technology trend that is likely to influence the enterprise environment up to and including 2025. Becoming foundational capabilities are intelligent automation, real-time analytics, distributed computing and immersive interfaces. Simultaneously, issues associated with trust, security, sustainability, and governance are becoming more strategic. This part will look into the greatest new enterprise technology trends, which will be sorted into thematic areas that will underscore how they impact strategically on future-ready organizations.

5.5.1 Intelligent and Autonomous Enterprise Systems

1. **Multimodal intelligence and Agentic AI emergence.**

   Artificial intelligence is no longer a slimmer, task-focused concept, but an agentic model that can independently think, plan, and carry out actions. The concept of agentic AI is intelligent software agents that are capable of recognizing objectives, breaking down complex tasks, communicating with digital worlds, and ameliorating results through repeated enhancement with limited human oversight. Multimodal AI expands this ability through the ability of the system to handle and integrate various types of data-text, images, audio, and structured data-in a single decision system.

   In the case of enterprises, this development is the shift between decision support and decision delegation. AI agents operating continuously and at scale have increasingly been augmented with customer service, supply chain orchestration, fraud detection, and clinical decision support. Companies that have implemented these capabilities have been enjoying faster, more personalized and resilient operations. Nevertheless, it is also true that the increasing autonomy of AI systems comes with new governance, accountability, and ethical issues, which have to be handled by strong governance frameworks.

2. **Intelligent Process Orchestration and Hyperautomation.**

   Hyperautomation is the next stage of automation in the enterprise, a combination of robotic process automation (RPA), machine learning, process mining, and low-code platforms to automate end-to-end business processes. Hyperautomation attempts to develop the self-optimizing business processes, which can be continuously improved, unlike previous automation efforts that concentrated on individual tasks.

Businesses are also using process mining solutions to detect workflow inefficiencies and workflow automation opportunities. Hyperautomation can be used to create dynamic workflows responding to evolving conditions when paired with AI-driven decision engines. It is not just cost reduction; there is also strategic value of better process quality, compliance and scalability. In the long run, Hyperautomation will be an inseparable element of the digital operating models.

3. **AI-Native Development and Platform Engineering.**

The AI-native tools and platform engineering practices are transforming software development itself. Automated testing systems, AI copilots and intelligent code generation are minimizing the time cycle of the development process and increasing the quality of the software. The field of platform engineering develops Internal Developer Platforms IDPs which provide application teams with standardized self-service development environments.

The platforms reduce infrastructure complexity while managing security and compliance and observability throughout the software delivery process. With the expansion of digital programs in businesses, platform engineering is proving critical in ensuring the productivity of developers, consistency of governance and operational stability. Any organization that invests in AI-enhanced development environments early will realize high benefits in terms of speed in innovations.

5.5.2 Hyperconnected Digital Infrastructure

A. **5G-Advanced and the Foundations of 6G.**

Next-generation connectivity is an essential facilitator of the digital enterprise transformation 5G-Advanced networks provide massive devices connectivity, high bandwidth, and ultra-low latency in real-time applications, including autonomous systems, remote operations and immersive collaboration. Some initial studies on 6G technologies have already taken place, and even more significant performance and novel communication paradigms are expected.

In the case of enterprises, there is a 5G network that is becoming a strategic resource in manufacturing, logistics, healthcare, and smart cities implementation. These networks provide determinism, improved security, and local control. To the extent that connectivity is becoming software-definable via network API, network infrastructure will experience a growing acceptance as a software-defined platform by enterprises.

AIoT and Edge Intelligence

The intersection of artificial intelligence and the Internet of Things - which is commonly known as AIoT - is changing physical processes into intelligent, data-driven systems. Edge computing is important because it processes data at the point of origin thereby lowering the latency, bandwidth use, and privacy concerns.

AIoT is being applied in industrial enterprises to facilitate predictive maintenance, real-time quality control and autonomous functions. In the medical field, edge AI is used in remote monitoring and point-of-care diagnostics. AIoT is used in smart cities to optimize traffic, manage energy, and protect citizens. The strategic implication is the development of never-ending sensing and responding business that can work in real time.

B. Digital Twins and Real-Time Simulation.

Digital twin technology Virtual simulations of real things or processes are quickly finding acceptance in the enterprise. Digital twins allow companies to track the performance, anticipate failures and optimize operations in the virtual world by means of sensor data, simulation models and analytics before such changes are introduced in the physical world.

The sectors that are actively involved with digital twin deployment are manufacturing, energy, healthcare, and urban infrastructure. Digital twins when combined with AI and edge computing will become real-time decision platforms that assist in predictive and prescriptive analytics. In the following years, digital twins will presumably be a common element of operational intelligence in the enterprise.

5.5.3 Trust, Security, and Responsible AI

1. **Zero Trust and Continuous Threat Exposure Management**

   The pattern of cybersecurity frameworks now exists within digital systems which use Zero Trust security systems to protect their internal networks. The Continuous Threat Exposure Management system (CTEM) expands this framework through its requirement of continuous threat assessment and active defense against security breaches. The use of artificial intelligence for threat detection together with extended detection and response systems and identity-based security measures has become standard practice in most organizations. Organizations are implementing password less authentication and passkey solutions to combat credential theft attacks. Future enterprise security systems will operate through ongoing system assessment which uses intelligent security methods instead of traditional perimeter defenses.

2. **AI Trust, Risk, and Security Management (AI TRiSM)**

   The quick implementation of artificial intelligence technology has increased worries about three specific issues, including bias, explainability, and privacy, and organizations must now follow regulatory standards. The development of AI TRiSM frameworks enables organizations to verify that their AI systems maintain trustworthiness and transparency while following ethical and legal requirements. The main elements of the system need to monitor models, detect biases, track data lineage, and use explainable artificial intelligence methods. Businesses worldwide are spending more money on artificial intelligence governance systems because regulatory requirements continue to change. Organizations that embed responsible AI practices early will achieve better results when they need to scale their AI operations while keeping their stakeholder trust.

5.5.4 Enterprise Blockchain and Tokenization

The current state of blockchain technology has progressed to develop enterprise-grade distributed ledger systems which exceed its initial function as a cryptocurrency network. The technology provides its most valuable applications through four main areas which include tokenizing physical assets and tracking supply chain origins and managing decentralized digital identities.

Different organizations in the finance and logistics and healthcare sectors use blockchain technology to improve transparency and decrease fraudulent activities and simplify their processes which involve multiple parties. The future effects of this situation will be determined by three factors which include standards for system interoperability and government regulations and current business systems integration.

5.5.5 Immersive and Experience-Centric Enterprise Platforms

i. **Spatial Computing and Extended Reality**

The field of spatial computing which includes augmented reality and virtual reality and mixed reality systems now moves from its experimental phase into full enterprise operational use. The technologies provide users with the ability to experience training programs through virtual environments and work together from different locations and create digital models and perform maintenance tasks with guided support. The workforce training solutions together with the complex equipment servicing requirements and design visualization needs make spatial computing systems essential for enterprise operations. The combination of decreasing hardware costs and advancing software development will lead to widespread use of immersive interfaces as the primary method of enterprise interaction.

ii. **Autonomous and Super Applications**

The development of smart applications now progresses toward creating autonomous software that can optimize itself and create personalized user experiences and deliver services without user input. The super app model which emerged in specific international markets now attracts growing interest from businesses that want to merge their various services into single digital platforms. The current developments demonstrate a wider trend which directs businesses to design their operations around customer experiences by developing systems that predict user requirements while managing service delivery through different networks. Businesses now gain competitive advantages through their ability to connect platforms with their data capabilities and their partnerships across different operational ecosystems.

5.5.6 Sustainable and Human-Centric Technology

A. **Climate Technology and Carbon-Aware Computing**

Sustainability has become a strategic goal for digital companies. Climate technology innovations create solutions that decrease carbon emissions through renewable energy deployment and energy-efficient computing and carbon-aware workload scheduling. Green data centers and sustainable cloud architectures are becoming more important in the current technological landscape. Organizations need to adopt sustainability metrics because of three main factors, which include their regulatory obligations and investor requirements and corporate environmental, social governance commitments. Carbon-aware computing enables systems to adjust their workload distribution according to current energy sources and emission levels which establishes a new standard for best practices.

B. **Human Augmentation and Connected Workforce**

The workforce now experiences productivity and safety improvements through advanced technologies which include neural interfaces and exoskeletons and wearable analytics and AI copilots. The augmented connected workforce model supports distributed and hybrid work environments through its three components which are real-time data and AI insights and collaboration tools. Organizations that implement wearable safety systems and AI productivity assistants and cognitive support tools achieve better results in both employee performance and health outcomes. The technology creates vital challenges which relate to privacy issues and workforce ethics and change management practices.

5.5.7 Frontier Computing Paradigms

1. **Quantum Computing**

   Quantum computing technology currently exists at a beginning phase which holds important strategic value for its future development. The technology can solve difficult optimization problems together with cryptographic challenges and molecular simulation tasks which will revolutionize multiple industries including pharmaceuticals and finance and materials science. Organizations today test hybrid quantum-classical systems together with cloud-based quantum computing solutions. Organizations should start their quantum readiness planning process because commercial quantum solutions will require several years to achieve their full market potential especially for cryptographic and high-performance analytics applications.

2. **Neuromorphic and Brain-Inspired Computing**

   The goal of neuromorphic computing research is to create computer systems which operate like the brain with low power consumption and intelligent learning capabilities. The research phase of this paradigm remains active yet it shows potential applications for edge intelligence and robotics and autonomous systems. The enterprise will benefit from its capacity to develop AI systems which work efficiently and learn continuously even with restricted resources. Technology-forward organizations should start their research activities through early monitoring of their research engagements.

5.5.8 Strategic Implications for Future Enterprises

The convergence of these emerging technologies signals a shift toward enterprises that are:

- **Autonomous** – driven by intelligent agents and Hyperautomation
- **Hyperconnected** – enabled by advanced networks and AIoT
- **Platform-centric** – built on internal and ecosystem platforms
- **Trust-driven** – governed by Zero Trust and responsible AI
- **Experience-focused** – powered by immersive and intelligent interfaces
- **Sustainable** – aligned with carbon-aware and ESG priorities
- **Continuously adaptive** – supported by real-time data and digital twins

Organizations that use these technologies without building connections between their different parts will create fragmented transformation results. The ability to combine different technologies into unified business functions and architectural design and governance development and organizations will determine their competitive advantage.

Digital transformation boundaries now face redefinition through emerging enterprise technology trends that shape enterprise operations. Enterprises will create intelligent systems that adapt and learn continuously instead of simply digitizing their current business processes. Agentic artificial intelligence, Hyperautomation, AIoT, spatial computing, and quantum research technologies create the basic elements needed for this transformation.

Organizations need to adopt all three digital technologies because technological adoption does not provide any guarantee of success. All enterprises need to find a balance between their innovative activities and the need to maintain control over their operations while they build secure systems that protect their sensitive data and create automated processes using human-centered design elements. The organizations that build strategic foresight and architectural discipline will achieve their digital transformation goals through ongoing capability development.

5.6 BUILDING A FUTURE-READY DIGITAL ENTERPRISE

Digital transformation has evolved beyond incremental technology upgrades into a comprehensive reconfiguration of how organizations create value, make decisions, and coordinate work. A future-ready digital enterprise is defined through its strategic alignment of technology platforms with organizational essential components such as strategy and human resources and business processes. Organizations that successfully navigate this shift transform their business functions from traditional support roles into key contributors that drive company development and protection against market changes. Organizations reach mature development when they create complete transformation programs which include both technological updates and organizational cultural development and organizational changes (Kristen Colella et al., 2025).

Building a future-ready enterprise requires organizations to establish a complete system perspective. Sustainable competitive advantages for businesses depend on technology investments which must be combined with their existing operational systems and their current data management systems and their unyielding corporate organizational practices. Enterprises that achieve superior performance through their entire transformation process develop their long-term strategic goals into actionable implementation capabilities. The established basic components of this enterprise system demonstrate how organizations achieve their digital transformation goals through their institutional framework which converts digital aspirations into business results.

5.6.1 Aligning Corporate Functions with Strategic Vision

The process of enterprise transformation faces its most challenging obstacle from functionally misaligned teams. The finance, human resources, marketing, and operations teams in multiple organizations function as separate entities which create their own local goals instead of supporting the organization's main strategic objectives. The digital enterprise needs these functions to work together through their shared purpose which follows the organization's long-term strategic goals.

The process of strategic alignment begins through the establishment of a future-back framework which shows the organization's goals. The leadership team must determine which functions will support organizational growth and innovation efforts while delivering customer value. The process requires the development of specific capability needs and process redesign projects and technology investments based on the strategic goals. This method enables organizations to create active business partners who help connect their strategic planning efforts with their daily operational work.

The shared responsibility systems need to be established as a critical requirement. Cross-functional collaboration frameworks, common performance metrics, and integrated planning cycles help ensure that functional priorities reinforce enterprise goals. Organizations that establish alignment mechanisms for their operations achieve better results in scaling their operations while adapting to market changes and maintaining their performance improvements over the long term.

5.6.2 Building Adaptive Organizational Capacity

An organization needs to develop its capacity for continuous adaptation to both technological disruptions and competitive challenges and changes in customer demands to achieve future readiness. The adaptive capacity of an organization describes its total ability to acquire new knowledge and implement organizational changes and deal with unexpected developments. Organizations develop their adaptable capabilities through implementing technological systems which establish operational flexibility but face restrictions because of organizational traditions and staff conduct.

Decision-making processes become less efficient because of fixed organizational structures and established operational procedures and employees who avoid taking risks. Organizations need to establish leadership practices and organizational customs that create an environment for exploration and staff empowerment and fast learning. The project requires the implementation of psychological safety measures that support team-based problem solving while providing recognition to team results instead of measuring their work output.

The workforce must be prepared for work. Employees need to develop their capacity for digital work and analytical tasks and collaboration abilities because business functions now require analytical skills and strategic abilities instead of traditional transactional work. Organizations must implement formal training programs to develop their staff and they should establish continuous learning frameworks to decrease resistance against organizational changes while increasing staff confidence about new work methods.

Organizations need to establish adaptive capacity as an ongoing operational ability which should become part of their core business functions. Organizations need to establish adaptive capacity as a permanent operational capability. Organizations that establish systems for ongoing education and feedback collection together with agile decision-making frameworks, develop the ability to maintain stability throughout periods of constant change.

5.6.3 Establishing a High-Quality Data Foundation

Data currently functions as the primary control system for modern digital businesses. The full value of data remains inaccessible to several organizations because their systems operate with incomplete data integration and they lack consistent data definitions and effective data management procedures. Advanced analytics and artificial intelligence (AI) and automation projects need solid data foundations to achieve their intended outcomes.

A future-ready enterprise treats data as a strategic product which operates through its essential business processes. The transition needs to implement controlled data management practices which operate through its four main components:

- **Data quality and timeliness:** The organization requires reliable standardized data which scientists continuously update to enable them to make decisions in real time while decreasing their need for reconciliation work.

- **Integrated data architecture:** Seamless flow of data transcending function breaks down silos and supports universal visibility across the enterprise.
- **Product mindset for data:** If the ownership, lifecycle management, and governance of data assets were structured explicitly, they could be made to align with business priorities.
- **Enterprise data literacy:** Building trust in data requires amplification in analytical capability, user confidingness in data source.

Organizations that invest in these capabilities receive operational and strategic advantages. The reporting process now requires only minutes to complete work that previously took several days because predictive analytics improves planning accuracy and AI-driven automation can now be implemented on large scales.The establishment of a reliable data system enables executives to move from traditional reporting methods to future-focused decision-making processes that create business value.

5.6.4 Strategic Embedding of Technology in Enterprise Functions

The implementation of digital tools results in inadequate outcomes for transformation initiatives because organizations choose to implement new technologies as additional components for their existing nonworking systems. Organizations need to modernize their entire workflows because automation should come after they finish the workflow redesign process. Organizations need to implement work redesign which enables them to achieve their goals through digital transformation that includes complete cloud computing and automation and AI implementation. The principle of design by exception serves as an effective guiding framework. The organizations need to determine their essential activities which create strategic differentiation and then proceed to implement customized solutions for those specific activities.

Organizations need to implement contemporary enterprise systems which enable them to create uniform automated workflows that will manage their entire business operations. The system enables the entire business to expand its operations while maintaining its unique market advantage through effective control of technical challenges.

Embedding the best science tends to naturally go through a series of disciplined steps.

1. Question the necessity of the existing processes.
2. Remove activities that are repetitive or low in value.
3. The remaining workflows need both simplification and optimization.
4. Structural improvements must first complete before we proceed with automation.

When technology investments are guided by business architecture rather than tool availability, corporate functions show measurable improvements through better cycle times and increased accuracy and improved insight generation. More important, technology transforms into a strategic agility enabler which creates extra operational difficulties.

5.6.5 Overcoming Architectural and Organizational Inertia

The primary challenge that many digital projects face stems from architectural inertia which innovation researchers define as the tendency of organizations to maintain their existing systems and procedures and their existing mental frameworks. The process of implementing new technologies into an organization without making necessary structural changes leads to organizational inertia becoming worse instead of getting better.

To overcome these constraints, enterprises need to implement changes that address both their organizational frameworks and their employee conduct. The primary implementation steps consist of the following key actions.

- Dissolving siloes by using platform-based operation models
- Redefining decision rights to accelerate execution

- Modernizing governance to support iterative delivery
- Aligning incentives with enterprise value creation
- Encouraging boundary-spanning collaboration

Leadership commitment plays a decisive role in this process. Executive leaders need to demonstrate required behaviour while working to achieve business results instead of improving their specific areas and they need to keep their attention on business operations after their first implementation work.

5.6.6 From Functional Efficiency to Enterprise Value Creation

Organizations have used efficiency measurements to evaluate their operational functions because these measurements assess their cost reduction capabilities and their ability to manage work processes. The digital enterprise of the future requires businesses to create value while generating insights and enabling strategic development. The finance function now develops into a more advanced role which uses predictive analytics to create future models and test different scenarios.The human resources department now focuses on building workforce capabilities instead of performing administrative tasks. Marketing has shifted from conducting campaigns to using data for understanding customer behavior. The organization develops new functional roles because of digital transformation which creates new business needs.

The enterprise platforms establish essential support for this transformation through their ability to deliver common data assets their development of uniform operational procedures and their integration of analytical tools. The organization can achieve better operational efficiency when the organization implements systems that enable all functions to work together through a unified digital infrastructure.

5.6.7 Integrating Vision, People, Process, and Technology

The defining characteristic of a future-ready digital enterprise is the tight integration of four foundational building blocks:

- **Vision** connects long-term strategic intent with near-term execution priorities.

- **People** provide the skills, behaviors, and leadership required for transformation.
- **Process** determines where work should be eliminated, optimized, or reinvented.
- **Technology and data** supply the scalable digital architecture that enables intelligent operations.

People who study organizations find that organizations achieve progress when they treat different elements as separate parts to be addressed individually. The sustainable transformation process requires all four aspects to develop simultaneously under effective governance and architectural control. Organizations need to become future-ready digital enterprises through complete organizational change that goes beyond technology implementation. The success of businesses depends on their ability to synchronize business operations with their strategic goals while developing flexibility and building reliable data systems and integrating technology into their new operational structures. Organizations that adopt this comprehensive strategy transform their business units into drivers of expansion and creativity. The company achieves operational efficiency through its approach, which combines vision and personnel and operational methods and technological systems. Future-ready organizations are equipped to transform their digital goals into ongoing business success because they operate in a world that experiences constant technological development and market competition.

5.7 SUMMARY

The chapter demonstrated how organizations need to develop their future-proof digital business operations through complete organizational changes that encompass their strategic direction and operational methods. Organizations need to align their three essential components which include their strategic vision and workforce and operational methods and technological systems to achieve sustainable digital success. The study showed that corporate functions need to transform from their current role as basic service providers into their future function as strategic partners who generate value through their support of data-based decision-making and business flexibility.

The chapter showed that organizations need to develop their capacity for adaptation while they need to eliminate their existing structural limitations and implement technological solutions after they rethink their operational processes. Organizations can improve their operational efficiency by using a single operating model which combines performance standards and key performance indicators and business systems. Businesses that implement a synchronized digital transformation process which starts from their future goals will achieve sustainable organizational growth and resilience and enduring market dominance in the digital business environment.

Multiple Choice Questions (MCQs)

1. **What is the primary purpose of value measurement in digital transformation?**
   A. To reduce employee workload
   B. To evaluate business outcomes and returns from investments
   C. To eliminate legacy systems completely
   D. To automate all business processes
2. **ROI (Return on Investment) is best described as:**
   A. Total revenue generated by a company
   B. Ratio of net profit to investment cost
   C. Number of customers acquired
   D. Cost of implementing technology
3. **Which of the following is a key component of business value assessment?**
   A. Employee attendance
   B. Financial, operational, and strategic benefits
   C. Office infrastructure
   D. Hardware specifications

4. **Continuous improvement models such as PDCA stand for:**
   A. Plan, Develop, Control, Assess
   B. Plan, Do, Check, Act
   C. Process, Design, Control, Analyze
   D. Plan, Deploy, Create, Automate

5. **Which of the following is a common KPI for measuring digital platform performance?**
   A. Number of office chairs
   B. System uptime and availability
   C. Office location
   D. Employee dress code

6. **What is the role of KPIs in enterprise platforms?**
   A. Replace employees
   B. Monitor and evaluate performance against goals
   C. Increase hardware costs
   D. Reduce customer engagement

7. **Which emerging technology is most associated with decentralized data management?**
   A. Cloud computing
   B. Blockchain
   C. Virtual machines
   D. ERP systems

8. **What is a key characteristic of a future-ready digital enterprise?**
   A. Rigid processes
   B. Manual workflows
   C. Agility and adaptability
   D. Limited data usage

9. **Which model focuses on iterative enhancement and feedback loops?**
   A. Waterfall model
   B. Continuous improvement model
   C. Linear model
   D. Static model
10. **Why are emerging enterprise technology trends important?**
    A. They increase operational costs
    B. They ensure organizations stay competitive and innovative
    C. They reduce customer satisfaction
    D. They eliminate all risks

Answers

1	2	3	4	5	6	7	8	9	10
B	B	B	B	B	B	B	C	B	B

References

1. Ahmed, E. M. (2024). *Developing Digital Inclusion Through Globalization and Digitalization.* https://doi.org/10.4018/979-8-3693-4111-7

2. Ardoq. (2024a). *What Is Enterprise Architecture (EA)? A Top Guide to Definition, Process, and Best Practices.*

3. Ardoq. (2024b). *What Is the Zachman Framework? A Definitive Guide to this EA Standard.*

4. Ardoq. (2024c). *What Is TOGAF? Definition and Uses of This Enterprise Architecture Framework.*

5. Barney, N., & Gillis, A. S. (2025). *IT applications, infrastructure and operations.*

6. BCG. (2022). *Business Model Innovation.*

7. Bhattacharjee, S. (2025). *What is Legacy Application Modernization?*

8. Boer, L. de. (2022). *What is the Operational Excellence Enterprise Readiness Model?*

9. Buchanan, I. (2025). *How do Agile and DevOps interrelate?*

10. Cataligent. (2025). *Drivers of Business Model Transformation.*

11. CATALYST. (2016). *Vision and Strategy Alignment.*

12. coursera. (2025). *What Are Performance Metrics?*

13. DynaTech Systems. (2024). *Navigating the Digital Transformation Maturity Model: A Comprehensive Framework for Future-Ready Enterprises.*

14. F.Dieffenbacher, S. (2022). *What is Digital Maturity, How to Measure, Tools & Models.*

15. Finesse, S. (2025). *What is a business value assessment, and why does it matter?*

16. Gallagher, N. (2025). *What is API management?*

17. Gaona, J. (2023). *What Is Platform Modernization?*

18. Geeksforgeeks. (2025a). *Cloud Computing Platforms and Technologies.*

19. Geeksforgeeks. (2025b). *Top 25 New Technology Trends in 2025.*

20. Geeksforgeeks. (2025c). *What is a KPI (Key Performance Indicator)?*

21. Grimm, A. (2025). *What Is a Partner Ecosystem? Importance and Examples.*

22. Harish. (2025). *Modernizing Business Processes for Digital Success.*

23. IBM. (2025a). *What is data integration?*

24. IBM. (2025b). *What is the Internet of Things (IoT)?*

25. Kristen Colella, Schmitt, R., & Seran, A. (2025). *Building future-ready functions with digital transformation for strategic growth.*

26. Lindemulder, G. (2025). *What is interoperability?*

27. Mitchell, T. (2025). *Tyler Mitchell.*

28. Monton, A. L. (2022). *Difference and Similarities: Digitization, Digitalization, and Digital Transformation.*

29. MyKase. (2026). *Digital transformation has become an existential imperative.*

30. Pitliya, G. (2025). *Strategic Roadmap to a Successful Digital Transformation Journey.*

31. Proctor, J. (2025). *The Value of Organizational Change Management Skills in AI-Enabled Organizations.*

32. Prosci. (2025). *Digital Transformation Maturity Model: A Complete Guide.*

33. Rehkopf, M. (2025). *The continuous improvement process: key steps, methodologies & benefits.*

34. Richards, A. (2015). *The Evolution of the Definitional Debate: The Policymaking Perspective.* https://doi.org/https://doi.org/10.1093/acprof:oso/9780198746966.003.0003

35. RMG. (2025). *Digital Transformation: Concept, Importance, and Benefits.*

36. SAP. (2025). *What is intelligent automation?*

37. Schwertner, K. (2025). *The Impact of Digital Transformation on Business: A Detailed Review.* https://doi.org/DOI: 10.51432/978-1-8381524-3-7_1

38. Shad. (2023). *Data Analytics and Decision Support Systems.*

39. Solution, S. (2023). *Digital Maturity, Digital Transformation.*

40. Stähler, P. (2026). *Business Model Innovation A fresh approach to strategy.*

41. Stryker, C. (2025). *What is artificial intelligence (AI)?*

42. Susnjara, S. (2024). *What is hybrid cloud architecture?*

43. SwissTech Solution. (2024). *Digitalization Strategies for Competitive Advantage.*

44. Theseira, D. (2024). *Guide to Common Enterprise Architecture Frameworks.*

45. vegam.ai. (2025). *Digital Transformation Governance Framework: Complete Guide.*

About the Authors

Manisha Ponugoti is an elite independent researcher and senior software engineer at the forefront of enterprise platform modernization. She specializes in transitioning complex legacy infrastructures into highly scalable, fault-tolerant microservice architectures. Her foundational work in the computer science field addresses critical industry bottlenecks through advanced API design, multi-cloud deployments, and the automation of high-volume, real-time data updates. Manisha's scalable solutions actively power critical operations used globally in over 60 countries and have served over one million end-users. Her research-backed implementations have demonstrably reduced legacy system transaction errors by 45% and accelerated service transaction speeds by 50%. As an author, she translates her highly specialized, practical findings into an authoritative guide for the software engineering industry, solidifying her position as a leading global voice in digital transformation.

Sandeepa Genne is an independent researcher and enterprise platform architect specializing in the design of scalable web and mobile systems for modern digital ecosystems. Her work centers on advancing enterprise platform modernization through cloud-native architectures, distributed systems, and high-performance cross-platform application frameworks. She focuses on solving critical challenges in large-scale environments, including secure web–mobile integration, real-time data synchronization, and API-driven platform scalability.

Her research explores emerging architectural paradigms such as micro-frontend ecosystems, event-driven service architectures, hybrid mobile frameworks, and multi-cloud platforms. She emphasizes building secure, resilient, and highly available infrastructures that support complex data workflows and large user bases while maintaining performance and reliability.

As an author, Sandeepa translates her practical expertise into actionable insights for the software engineering community, contributing thought leadership to the evolving field of enterprise platform engineering and digital transformation.

www.ingramcontent.com/pod-product-compliance
Lightning Source LLC
LaVergne TN
LVHW022203200926
848481LV00006B/1828
9798904315436